Forty Years Later

God's Faithfulness Across Generations

Mary L. Lyon

InspiringVoices®

Scripture quotations taken from the New American Standard Bible®,
Copyright © 1960, 1962, 1963, 1968, 1971, 1972, 1973, 1975, 1977, 1995
by The Lockman Foundation. Used by permission. (www.Lockman.org)

Inspiring Voices books may be ordered through booksellers or by contacting:

Inspiring Voices
1663 Liberty Drive
Bloomington, IN 47403
www.inspiringvoices.com
1 (866) 697-5313

ISBN: 978-1-4624-1089-7 (sc)
ISBN: 978-1-4624-1090-3 (e)

Library of Congress Control Number: 2014921783

Printed in the United States of America.

Inspiring Voices rev. date: 12/22/2014

CONTENTS

JOSEPH

OTHER WITNESSES

WE ARE HIS GOOD WORK

DEDICATION

There are many people who have been a part of my Christian
journey. People who have been gracious and patient with
this sinner learning to walk with God. I am grateful to
all of you and dedicate this book to you. Thank you for
sharing yourselves with me and standing by me.

ACKNOWLEDGEMENT

In every endeavor there are those who labor in love to support those of us who pursue our dreams. I am blessed by those who have labored in love with me. Each of them used their gifts to help me.

NB – The hours we have spent discussing the message of these chapters have been a blessing in my life and hopefully, will be a blessing in the lives of those who read this book. Thank you for your faithfulness and prayers.

BK – Your faith in me has helped me through the doubts and questions. Everyone needs someone like you in their life. Thank you for listening to me and laughing with me.

TC – Thank you for all your help and advice. I look forward to reading your book.

RS – As you have walked with me through God's latest lessons for me, it has influenced these pages. You are gifted. Your faithfulness to our Lord with your gifts is an encouragement to me. Thank you.

AJ – Thank you for your continued help and sharing of your gifts. You are a very talented person.

CT – Thank you for offering to proofread these pages. I so appreciate your generous gift. Your input was helpful.

Inspiring Voices – You continue to give me good advice and help me fulfill my dream. Thank you for the role you had in making this book a reality.

Finally, this book would not be possible without the guidance of the Spirit of God. The pages that follow are about what God accomplishes in the life of His children. God is ever faithful to His children and accomplishes His purposes. To Him be all the glory.

FOREWORD

"When she speaks she has something worthwhile to say, and she always says it kindly." ~ Proverbs 31:26

This verse is synonymous with who Mary Lyon is. She is a friend that every woman desires to have in her posse. She is Jesus with skin on, a developer of holiness. She's a woman that lives to encourage and inspire other women in their walks with Jesus. She is servant-hearted, and has dedicated her life to serving others.

Mary shares in her book, *Forty Years Later, God's Faithfulness Across Generations*, how God is faithful to finish His divine purpose in each of our lives. She shares insights on how we can attain that plan by trusting His faithfulness toward us.

Mary also blogs about grace and faith at www.hewalkswithus.com.

Teresa Coelho
Power of Modesty
www.powerofmodesty.com

INTRODUCTION

"For the flesh sets its desires against the Spirit,
and the Spirit against the flesh; for these
are in opposition to one another, so that you
may not do the things that you please."
Galatians 5:17

As God walks with me, I struggle with wanting to be in submission to Him and yet wanting my circumstances to be different. There is a part of me that so wants to do the will of God and another part of me that so wants my will. The struggle described in Galatians 5:17 is real in God's walk with me.

God always gets me through these struggles and the process by which He does it fascinates me. Studying the trials of biblical characters is always a source of strength and encouragement for me as I seek to understand my struggles. God's faithfulness in their lives helps me understand what He is trying to accomplish in my life.

I am not discussing the trials that come with crisis, but the struggles with day to day living. It is hard. The struggles are real and God's faithfulness to walk with us through the struggles is real. And sometimes, I feel defeated in the midst of the battle. Yet, God faithfully brings me through to victory.

This book is about what God has taught me and is teaching me in the midst of these struggles. This book is about how God faithfully leads us through a wilderness journey as we learn to trust Him in the midst of the struggles.

I believe we all need a wilderness journey experience of struggling in God's walk with us. I derive this concept of a wilderness journey experience from the forty years the Israelites spent in the wilderness before entering and taking possession of the Promised Land. God was faithful to His promise across generations when He brought the Israelites into the Promised Land. The Israelites, however, first needed to spend forty years in the wilderness learning to trust God.

It is in the wilderness that we gain a personal experiential knowledge of God. We find that He is so much more interested in the process of developing Christ in us than the end result. Actually, the end result is decided – we will one day be fully like Him and with Him. As we live in this world, it is a labor of God's love to work Christ in us.

I believe God has a plan for each of us and the wilderness journey is part of the plan. I also believe there is a work for each of us and the wilderness journey process prepares us for the work. What we are doing today is only preparing us for tomorrow.

Joseph is my favorite example of how God uses a wilderness experience. There is something about his life and service to the Lord that is unique and special. His wilderness story teaches us that bad things can happen even when we do the right thing. His story also teaches us that God has a plan in all that we encounter, good and bad, through the course of our lives.

A wilderness experience I have always feared is one like the wilderness experience of the biblical character, Job. Well, I survived my Job experience and have new appreciation for this biblical person and God's comfort in sorrow. He is a very loving God.

I hope as we look at the wilderness journeys and lives of biblical people of faith that you will be encouraged to read more and learn more from their lives. Their lives and their stories are rich with God's faithfulness in His relationship with His chosen. There is so much more to their lives than what I have shared. They are friends in Christ.

I hope the truths laid out in this book will help you in your wilderness journey and help you to help others on their journeys.

CHAPTER 1

CLOUD OF WITNESSES

"Therefore, since we have so great a cloud of
witnesses surrounding us, let us also lay aside every
encumbrance, and the sin which so easily entangles
us, and let us run with endurance the race that is
set before us, fixing our eyes on Jesus, the author
and perfecter of faith, who for the joy set before Him
endured the cross, despising the shame, and has sat
down at the right hand of the throne of God."
Hebrews 12:1, 2

The Christian life is a lifelong journey with the wilderness experience being a part of it. It is a journey we need to be prepared to take. When undergoing any journey, a person has a checklist of needed items. For our journeys, God has provided a cloud of witnesses to provide us with the hope we need to persevere.

I just finished the book, *Blind Descent* by Brian Dickinson, which exemplifies this value of the testimony of others who have gone before us. The book tells his story as he ascends to the summit of Mount Everest, only to have to descend blind. As he prepared for his climb, he studied other climbs and climbers. As he climbed, he could see the paths taken by other climbers. Ultimately, it was God's faithfulness that brought him safely home.

The cloud of witnesses mentioned in Hebrews 11 help us on the path God will have us take to His summit. And often, we will feel blind in our steps of faith. God, however, will be faithful.

We need these witnesses. We need to study their journeys. God gave us their stories to encourage us. Here is what the author of Hebrews says these witnesses tell us:

> *"Now faith is the assurance of things hoped*
> *for, the conviction of things not seen. For by*
> *it the men of old gained approval."*
> *Hebrews 11:1, 2*

And,

> *"And without faith it is impossible to please Him, for*
> *he who comes to God must believe that He is, and*
> *that He is a rewarder of those who seek Him"*
> *Hebrews 11:6*

Our witnesses teach us that God wants people who will have faith in Him. He wants people who will believe in Him. Our witnesses also show us that they found Him faithful; that He rewards those who seek Him. As we study their lives, we see the faithfulness of God to His promises and to His people. God's faithfulness was the source of their faith and is the source of our faith.

Why is their witness important? To help us lay aside those encumbrances and sins that get in the way of us having faith. Their faith encourages our faith. The journeys they endured give us strength and hope to endure our journeys. The Hebrews author actually calls it a race. The Apostle Paul used this same expression:

"Do you not know that those who run in a race all run,
but only one receives the prize? Run in such a way that
you may win. And everyone who competes in the games
exercises self-control in all things. They then do it to
receive a perishable wreath, but we an imperishable.
Therefore I run in such a way, as not without aim; I
box in such a way, as not beating the air; but I buffet
my body and make it my slave, lest possibly, after I have
preached to others, I myself should be disqualified."
1 Corinthians 9:24-27

Paul is talking about self-discipline that lays aside 'every encumbrance and the sin that so easily entangles us.' When athletes train for a race they have strict dos and don'ts that they follow especially if they want to win. Paul and the author of Hebrews is telling us that we need to be disciplined in our Christian training in faith.

We need this cloud of witnesses to encourage us to stay disciplined on our journeys as we grow in our faith in God's walk with us. The stories of these witnesses let us see how God works in the lives of His people. We see how their experiences built up their faith in God. We see His faithfulness in their lives.

By studying biblical characters, we gain an understanding of what God wants to accomplish in our lives through circumstances, relationships and events we experience. He had these stories written, so we could have faith in Him. He had these stories written, so we could have hope that just as He was faithful to them He will be faithful to us.

God wants us to know that He is a faithful God. God wants us to experience His faithfulness in our daily lives.

CHAPTER 2

THE WILDERNESS

"But He Himself would often slip away
to the wilderness and pray."
Luke 5:16

Jesus would slip away to the wilderness to pray. Jesus met with His Father in the wilderness. If Jesus felt the need to spend time in the wilderness to meet with our Heavenly Father, then we need time in the wilderness to meet with our Heavenly Father.

It is in the wilderness, through experiences in the wilderness, that we come to know God for who He is. God walks with us and leads us in the wilderness. He brings us to a place in our faith that we truly are able to say with the Apostle Paul:

> *"I have been crucified with Christ; and it is no longer*
> *I who live, but Christ lives in me; and the life which I*
> *now live in the flesh I live by faith in the Son of God,*
> *who loved me, and delivered Himself up for me."*
> *Galatians 2:20*

When I think of lives that learned not to live in the flesh but by faith in God as Paul describes, I think of the wilderness journey of the Israeli nation. The Israeli nation had to wander in the wilderness for forty years, because the parents, who lived according to the flesh, refused to enter the Promised Land. Forty years later, after learning to trust God in the wilderness, after learning to live by faith, the children entered the Promised Land.

It was in the wilderness that God tested and trained His chosen ones, the Israeli people, as part of His perfect plan for them to enter and possess the Promised Land. In the wilderness, they only had God in whom to trust. Like them, we too, need wilderness journeys to learn to trust God, first and foremost, so we can possess His promises as His children.

By studying the wilderness experience of the Israeli nation and the wilderness journeys of other biblical characters, we observe the faithfulness of God. We discover that God's work in the hearts of His chosen people involves years of toil. We see the beauty of the wilderness journey in building faith in God's chosen ones.

God choosing us is an amazing gift. His patience toward us, in the wilderness, as we learn to have faith in Him is overwhelming. God is committed to building faith in us. He wants us to fully enjoy His presence in our lives.

This work of faith is not easy. The wilderness is not an easy journey. It is not an overnight camping trip. The Israeli nation spent 40 years in the wilderness. I believe Abraham spent 25 years. Jacob spent 20 years. It takes time and adversity to build a people strong in faith in the Lord.

The wilderness journey is very much about struggling in faith and God being faithful to His work in His chosen ones. Biblical characters struggled. They failed. They learned faith. They learned that God is faithful. The real message of the wilderness is that God is faithful to His promises and His children across generations. His faithfulness is the foundation for our faith.

The Apostle Paul describes our struggling in the wilderness and the struggling of biblical characters:

> *"For that which I am doing, I do not understand; for*
> *I am not practicing what I would like to do, but I am*
> *doing the very thing I hate. Wretched man that I am!*
> *Who will set me free from the body of this death?"*
> Romans 7:15, 24

Paul immediately follows those verses by stating how we find the victory to the struggling:

> *"Thanks be to God through Jesus Christ our Lord!"*
> Romans 7:25

God has given us victory in Jesus Christ. Romans 8:10, 11 describe the Holy Spirit as the power for our faith in God's faithfulness in our struggling. The Spirit gives us life to live as God asks as we grow in faith.

Just as biblical characters learned to trust God through struggling in the wilderness, we learn to trust God through struggling in the wilderness. And, as our faith in God's faithfulness grows, as the Apostle Paul described, we more fully experience the Spirit of God giving us life. What a beautiful promise.

CHAPTER 3

THE JOURNEY OUT

"And the priests who carried the ark of the covenant
of the Lord stood firm on dry ground in the middle of
the Jordan while all Israel crossed on dry ground, until
all the nation had finished crossing the Jordan."
Joshua 3:17

While this book is about wilderness experiences, it's important to remember that God does not abandon us to the wilderness. He will faithfully fulfill His promises concerning us just as He has for all His chosen.

The Israelites entered the Promised Land. Abraham received an heir. Christ came and died for the penalty for our sins. God will accomplish His promises concerning us.

To leave the wilderness and enter the Promised Land, the Israelites had to trust God to provide a path on dry land through the Jordan River. God did provide a path. Abraham, in His test of faith, had to trust God for a substitute sacrifice for his son. God did provide a substitute. God is always faithful.

When I left what I call my wilderness journey, I had to trust God through a very painful time. God had a very special way for me to leave the wilderness. Leaving the wilderness is not the end. In so many ways, it is the beginning of a deeper walk with God.

While my Jordan River crossing was painful, it was also full of God's presence, love and comfort. Just as the Israelites had to trust that God would hold the water back as they crossed the Jordan so that they would not drown, I had to trust God that I would not drown in the pain. And, just as the Israelites had each other to support them in their faith, God has given me faithful friends to encourage me in my faith. God has been with me each step of the way. God is faithful.

As I stated earlier, whenever I thought about God's walk with me, the biblical story of Job always scared me. I did not want a Job experience in my relationship with the Lord. A lot of the stories of God using people in the Bible overwhelm me, but none like Job.

In Job 1:6-11, the sons of God present themselves to God. God has a conversation with Satan about Job. God proceeds to give permission to Satan to do whatever he wants to Job, but he cannot touch Job. Satan proceeds to have Job's family killed and Job robbed of all his possessions. Job had ten children (plus spouses and children) that he lost as well as his servants and stock. It was devastating. The author of Job tells us:

> *"Through all this Job did not sin nor did he blame God."*
> *Job 122*

There is another day when the sons of God present themselves and God and Satan again discuss Job. This time God gives Satan permission to harm Job and he does:

> *"Then Satan went out from the presence of the Lord, and smote Job with sore boils from the sole of his foot to the crown of his head."*
> *Job 2:7*

In God's walk with me, I really was not seeking that kind of attention. People would say, but God blessed Job so much more at the end of the story. Yes, God did. I still did not want the attention. Yet, it is how I feel my wilderness journey ended. I do believe it has been my experience in crossing my Jordan River.

God has always prepared me when He would have my life take a new direction, so He prepared me for the River crossing. I knew change was coming. My biggest fear in thinking about what the change might be was that he would take my cousin, whom I had lived with for 9 years and had medically cared for most of those years, home with Him. I would pray that God would have mercy on me and heal her. It was not a loss I wanted to bear.

In November, 2014, I took her to the emergency room with a very bad blood infection. She was not expected to live 48 hours let alone 24. I prayed through Psalms 23.

God had mercy on me and I brought her home. It wasn't easy with drug infusion therapy of antibiotics and other drugs, but she was alive and she was home. I was so grateful to the Lord.

However, things did take a turn at work and I had to make a decision. As I said, I knew change was coming and it became clear to me that resigning from my job was something God wanted me to do. While it was a painful process for me, I did feel some relief because I thought it meant that my cousin would live. Resigning my job was the new direction, right? Okay, loss of a job is not great but the better alternative.

Then God spoke in the stillness of my heart and told me that He was going to take my cousin home with Him. He was not going to heal her in the way I wanted. He would give me some time with her and then He would heal her by taking her home.

And while I hoped I heard God wrong, I prayed for His strength and comfort as I lived out the next few days, months....I did not know how long...of my cousin's life.

While I did everything I could to comfort and help her fight to live, I knew God was taking her home. When the day came to make the decision to stop the fight, we made it together. I held her hand and said I would be with her until the end and I was. God gave us a special time together.

I asked God to please let me know when she saw His face and joined Him in heaven. I will never forget holding her hand and seeing her eyes open and her mouth smile. God let me be present as He took her home.

If only that was the end of the story. Remember, Job was touched in three ways: family, finances and self. I had lost my job and my cousin had died. I remember telling God that that was enough loss for me. And while I cannot say I experienced more loss, I can say that I found myself having to take probably my biggest steps of faith.

Since I am on the other side of the pain, it is hard to explain just how painful it was. I describe it as God removing the scar tissue from injuries of the past. I borrowed this description from an infection I needed to have cleaned.

I once had an infected staph infection. The doctor used a scalpel to open the wound and squeeze out the infection. Unbeknownst to me when he started was that I would feel it all. This pretty much is how it felt as God opened up old emotional wounds and removed the infection. I remember not being able to stand up straight when the doctor was done. I had more pain than when I came. But, as I healed I saw the wisdom in the process used by the doctor. As I heal, I see God's wisdom in the process of healing old wounds.

I am truly blessed because my friends stood by me. I had to face my fears and, more importantly, my greatest fears. But, I live in the joy of victory.

A friend commented that she did not feel that I ever hit the depths of despair. I responded that God held my heart and my hand through it all. He walked with me through the pain and loss. He embraced me and held me with more love than I have ever known. God tenderly touched me through dear friends.

I do not believe I could have experienced the power of the moment with my cousin or appreciated the beauty of what God was doing in my life, if I had not been through the wilderness and experienced God's great love toward me.

The wilderness prepared me for that moment when I participated with God welcoming one of His children home, my cousin. The wilderness prepared me to face my greatest fears. I am thankful for what God has done in my life in the wilderness.

As you read the words that follow, as I try to describe the breadth and depth of the wilderness experiences God uses to deepen His walk with us, as we study these biblical examples, please remember that I too have experienced the loss and the pain, BUT, also the victory and the joy. I close with:

> *"Thou, in Thy great compassion, Didst not forsake*
> *them in the wilderness; The pillar of cloud did not*
> *leave them by day, To guide them on their way, Nor the*
> *pillar of fire by night, to light for them the way in which*
> *they were to go. And Thou didst give Thy good Spirit*
> *to instruct them, Thy manna Thou didst not withhold*
> *from their mouth, And Thou didst give them water for*
> *their thirst. Indeed, forty years Thou didst provide for*
> *them in the wilderness and they were not in want."*
> *Nehemiah 9:19-21*

ISRAELI NATION

"Now it came about in the course of those many days that the king of Egypt died. And the sons of Israel sighed because of the bondage, and they cried out; and their cry for help because of their bondage rose up to God. So God heard their groaning; and God remembered His covenant with Abraham, Isaac, and Jacob. And God saw the sons of Israel, and God took notice of them."
Exodus 2:23-25

CHAPTER 4

STORY

*"The land of Egypt is at your disposal; settle your father
and your brothers in the best of the land, let them live in
the land of Goshen; and if you know any capable men
among them, then put them in charge of my livestock."*
Genesis 47:6

Genesis 47:6 was spoken to Joseph (Jacob's son) by the Pharaoh
when Jacob (Israel) and his family moved to Egypt. There was a
great famine in the land and under Joseph's leadership, Egypt was
the one nation with supplies to help other nations survive. Jacob
and the family moved to Egypt to survive the famine under the
provision of Joseph.

We pick up the story after several hundred years have passed
since these words were spoken. Here is the Biblical description of the
condition of the Israeli nation in Egypt four hundred plus years later:

*"Now a new king arose over Egypt, who did not know
Joseph. And he said to his people, "Behold, the people
of the sons of Israel are more and mightier than we.
Come, let us deal wisely with them, lest they multiply*

*and in the event of war, they also join themselves to
those who hate us, and fight against us, and depart
from the land." So they appointed taskmasters over
them to afflict them with hard labor. And they built
for Pharaoh storage cities, Pithom and Raames."*
Exodus 1:8-11

As the nation kept multiplying, the Egyptians kept piling on the adversity. The Israeli's numbers got to a level that the Pharaoh required the midwives to kill all the sons born to Israel. The midwives however, feared the Lord and did not do as Pharaoh requested. The Pharaoh was committed to this deed and thus, commanded his people to throw the newborn sons of the Israelites into the Nile.

One Israeli mother to save her three month old son hid him in a basket and placed the basket in the Nile. She watched as Pharaoh's daughter rescued the basket. Pharaoh's daughter named him Moses and raised him Egyptian. However, Moses' heart was with his relatives, the Israelites. Moses actually killed an Egyptian to defend some Israelites which led him to flee to the wilderness.

After 40 years in the wilderness, Moses received his call from God and returned to Egypt to lead the Israeli nation to the land God promised Abraham, Isaac and Jacob. After plagues and other disasters, Moses successfully led the nation out of Egypt.

As the Israelites fled the Egyptians, it became necessary to part the Red Sea. The Biblical story provides the reason for the path taken by the nation that led to the Red Sea:

*"Now when it came about when Pharaoh had let
the people go, that God did not lead them by the
way of the land of the Philistines, even though it was
near; for God said, "Lest the people change their
minds when they see war, and they return to Egypt.
Hence God led the people around by the way of the*

wilderness to the Red Sea; and the sons of Israel
went up in martial array from the land of Egypt."
Exodus 13:17, 18

The nation passed through the Red Sea on dry land with walls
of water on both sides of them. When the Egyptians followed the
walls of water engulfed them. It's interesting that the nation had to
pass through water for their salvation from the Egyptians (I think
of water baptism). The Red Sea which led to life for the children of
God, led to death for the enemies of God's children. That which God
used to save the nation was damnation for her enemies.

As the nation travelled to the Promised Land, the Ten
Commandments were given to the people and the tabernacle erected.
God resided in the tabernacle as He led the nation. As the nation
camped in the wilderness of Paran (Numbers 12:16), men were sent
to spy out the Promised Land.

Only a couple of years had passed since the nation left Egypt
and the spies were sent into the Promised Land. When the spies
returned, they spoke well of the land, but communicated fear of the
inhabitants. Here is the spies report:

> *"Thus they told him, and said, 'We went in to the*
> *land where you sent us; and it certainly does flow*
> *with milk and honey, and this is its fruit.'... 'We*
> *are not able to go up against the people, for they are*
> *too strong for us...we became like grasshoppers in*
> *our own sight, and so we were in their sight.'"*
> *Numbers 13:27-33*

Because of their fear of the inhabitants, the nation refused to
enter the Promised Land and God passed judgment:

> *"Say to them, 'As I live,' says the Lord, 'just as you*
> *have spoken in My hearing, so I will surely do to you;*

> *your corpses shall fall in this wilderness, even all your*
> *numbered men, according to your complete number*
> *from twenty years old and upward, who have grumbled*
> *against Me....Your children, however, whom you said*
> *would become a prey - I will bring them in, and they*
> *shall know the land which you have rejected. And your*
> *sons shall be shepherds for forty years in the wilderness,*
> *and they shall suffer for your unfaithfulness...According*
> *to the number of days which you spied out the land,*
> *forty days, for every day you shall bear your guilt a year,*
> *even forty years, and you shall know My opposition.'"*
> Numbers 14:28-34

The Israeli nation returned to wandering in the wilderness because of their lack of faith in God. They feared man more than they feared God. God in His faithfulness stayed with them in the wilderness. Forty years later, new spies were sent to spy out the land and here is their report:

> *"And they said to Joshua, 'Surely the Lord has given*
> *all the land into our hands, and all the inhabitants of*
> *the land, moreover, have melted away before us.'"*
> Joshua 2:24

What a contrast in reports. What happened to being grasshoppers? The wilderness happened. God did a work of faith in the lives of the people of the nation of Israel in the wilderness.

CHAPTER 5

WILDERNESS

"By faith they passed through the Red Sea as
though they were passing through dry land; and the
Egyptians, when they attempted it, were drowned."
Hebrews 11:29

I love that the nation had to pass through water. I think of John
the Baptist who came baptizing in water saying that people must
repent because the kingdom of God was at hand. God was about to
do great things for the nation of Israel. But first, they needed to be
baptized by water and have a wilderness experience. It is interesting
that right after Christ was baptized, He was led into the wilderness.

To understand what happened to the Israeli nation in the
wilderness, we need to understand the history of the parents who
died in the wilderness. Their story helps us understand the work
God accomplished in the wilderness in the lives of the children who
would possess the Promised Land.

Parents

The parents were born slaves and had only known slavery for their entire lives. They had been oppressed and bore great adversity until the nation's exodus out of Egypt. The Bible story does not give us any indication that during the four hundred years of slavery that God communicated with them. We can assume they knew of God's promises because they knew to take Joseph's bones with them (Exodus 13:19). However, it appears that they have no personal experiential knowledge of God and His faithfulness to His promises.

Then, one day, Moses came to them and told them that 'I AM' (Exodus 3:14) has sent him to deliver them. Moses will stand up to the Pharaoh with a staff (a staff was appropriate since it was used by a shepherd to lead his sheep) and demand that the Pharaoh let God's people go. I can only imagine what the Israelites thought.

The deliverance of the nation was accomplished as God promised. The nation left Egypt and headed for the Promised Land. Of course, they encountered the Red Sea first and complained to Moses. God showed His power to deliver His people and parted the Red Sea.

On the journey, the people grumbled about bitter water and God answered. They complained about hunger and God provided manna. They complained about the lack of water and God provided water. Are you seeing a pattern?

Whenever there would be an obstacle or a delay, the nation would grumble. And God, patiently, would demonstrate His faithfulness. The nation would only be content until the next obstacle or delay. The nation just could not trust in faith in God's provision for their every need. They struggled with knowing God as their faithful God.

So, when the spies see the great land that God wants to give them, they also see the great people who live in the land. Let's look again at what they reported:

> *"...we became like grasshoppers in our own*
> *sight, and so we were in their sight."*
> Numbers 13:33

Notice the pattern to the statement: 'we became like grasshoppers in our own sight' and 'so we were in their sight.' The negative thought started with the Israelites. And because they believed the thought about themselves, they believed the other nations believed it about them.

The parents were not looking to God as the one to fight the battles, but themselves. And, because they saw themselves fighting the battles, they were very afraid. Their lack of faith in God to fight and win the battles for them caused them to let their fear make the decision. Out of fear they chose not to enter the Promised Land. It required faith, which they lacked, to enter into His promise.

Story of the Children in the Wilderness

As we consider the children whose faith was trained in the wilderness, I am talking primarily about the children borne into slavery who have been on this trip with the parents. They have experiential knowledge from whence they have come. They have memories of being slaves.

These children also experienced the parting of the Red Sea, the giving of the Ten Commandments and the building of the tabernacle. They also know about their parents' refusal to enter the Promised Land.

They saw their parents die in the wilderness for their lack of faith. They lived out God's judgment of forty years in the wilderness. They have a much different story than their parents.

Yes, the children started out as slaves, but they lived the majority of their lives wandering in the wilderness trusting God. As we look at the children's experience in the wilderness, we see that God led them,

He disciplined them, He provided for them, and He trained them. Let's look at what life in the wilderness was like for the children.

God led the children and guided them every day and every night:

> *"Now on the day that the tabernacle was erected the cloud covered the tabernacle, the tent of the testimony, and in the evening it was like the appearance of fire over the tabernacle, until morning. So it was continuously; the cloud would cover it by day, and the appearance of fire by night. And whenever the cloud was lifted from over the tent, afterward the sons of Israel would then set out; and in the place where the cloud settled down, there the sons of Israel would camp. At the command of the Lord the sons of Israel would set out, and at the command of the Lord they would camp; as long as the cloud settled over the tabernacle, they remained camped...At the command of the Lord they camped, and at the command of the Lord they set out; they kept the Lord's charge, according to the command of the Lord through Moses."*
> *Numbers 9:15-23*

The children experienced forty years of following the leadership of their Lord and God. God directed their steps and their travels. He determined the path they would travel and when they would travel. He was faithfully in control of their wilderness journey.

The children had a physical representation of God leading them. It was not just something to believe, but they could see it in the cloud and fire that would cover the tabernacle. God was very present with them.

God disciplined for disobedience:

God was raising up a people to follow Him. He had standards for their conduct and behavior toward Him and toward each other.

> *"Now while the sons of Israel were in the wilderness,*
> *they found a man gathering wood on the Sabbath day.*
> *And those who found him gathering wood brought him to*
> *Moses and Aaron, and to all the congregation; and they*
> *put him in custody because it had not been declared what*
> *should be done to him. Then the Lord said to Moses, "The*
> *man shall surely be put to death; all the congregation*
> *shall stone him with stones outside the camp.""*
> *Numbers 15:32-35*

God had the nation participate in the discipline. He wanted them to feel the same anger for sin that He did. He desired for them to desire holiness in their midst. It is interesting what happens when sin is tolerated. God wanted His children to learn to not tolerate sin.

> *"Then they set out from Mount Hor by the way of the*
> *Red Sea, to go around the land of Edom; and the people*
> *became impatient because of the journey. And the people*
> *spoke against God and Moses, 'Why have you brought*
> *us up out of Egypt to die in the wilderness? For there*
> *is no food and no water, and we loathe this miserable*
> *food.' And the Lord sent fiery serpents among the people*
> *and they bit the people, so that many people of Israel*
> *died. So the people came to Moses and said, "We have*
> *sinned, because we have spoken against the Lord and*
> *you; intercede with the Lord, that He may remove the*
> *serpents from us." And Moses interceded for the people.*
> *Then the Lord said to Moses, "Make a fiery serpent,*
> *and set it on a standard; and it shall come about, that*
> *everyone who is bitten, when he looks at it, he shall live.""*
> *Numbers 21:4-7*

The story in Numbers 24:1-7 is often referred to as an example of what the cross means to believers in Christ. Just as the Israelites looked to the serpent Moses made to be healed, Christians look to the cross to be healed of the sting of sin and death.

Here is what I like about God's solution of having a standard provided to which the Israelites could focus their faith. God required the exercise of faith on the part of the people. God could have simply removed the serpents. Instead, God provided an opportunity for the people to exercise faith and turn to the standard and be healed.

> *"While Israel remained at Shittim, the people began*
> *to play the harlot with the daughters of Moab. For*
> *they invited the people to the sacrifices of their gods,*
> *and the people ate and bowed down to their gods.*
> *So Israel joined themselves to Baal of Peor, and the*
> *Lord was angry against Israel. And the Lord said to*
> *Moses, "Take all the leaders of the people and execute*
> *them in broad daylight before the Lord, so that the*
> *fierce anger of the Lord may turn away from Israel"...*
> *And those who died by the plague were 24,000."*
> Numbers 25:1-9

That is serious discipline. God was serious when He said they would have no other gods before Him. He expected them to understand that there is only one true God and it was Him. He expected obedience to His commands.

God continued to provide for the children throughout the journey with manna and water:

God made sure they had the food they needed, the protection they needed, and the shelter they needed. He made provision.

> *"And the manna ceased on the day after they had*
> *eaten some of the produce of the land, so that the sons*

> *of Israel no longer had manna, but they ate some of*
> *the yield of the land of Canaan during that year."*
> Joshua 5:12

Once the nation entered the Promised Land, they no longer needed the manna that God provided day after day. God now provided through the abundance in the land they would possess.

God prepared the children for battle and let them taste victory at His hands:

> "When the Canaanite, the king of Arad, who lived in
> the Negev, heard that Israel was coming by the way of
> Atharim, then he fought against Israel, and took some of
> them captive. So Israel made a vow to the Lord, and said,
> "If Thou wilt indeed deliver this people into my hand,
> then I will utterly destroy their cities." And the Lord heard
> the voice of Israel, and delivered up the Canaanites;
> then they utterly destroyed them and their cities."
> Numbers 21:1-3

> "But Sihon would not permit Israel to pass through his
> border. So Sihon gathered all his people and went out
> against Israel in the wilderness, and came to Jahaz and
> fought against Israel. Then Israel struck him with the
> edge of the sword, and took possession of his land from
> the Arnon to the Jabbok, as far as the sons of Ammon;
> for the border of the sons of Ammon was Jazer. And
> Israel took all these cities and Israel lived in all the cities
> of the Amorites, in Heshbon, and in all her villages."
> Numbers 21:23-25

These are simple shepherds who are having victory in battle. They are learning to fight. But more importantly, they are learning to trust God to give them victory in battle. They are learning to have courage in the face of fear.

We have an amazing snapshot of the wilderness journey of the children. Forty years of God leading them, providing for them, disciplining them and giving them victory in battle before they send in their own spies. They are prepared to trust God by entering the Promised Land and conquering the inhabitants.

The children's faith to enter the Promised Land is a contrast to the parents. The parents, however, did not have the experience of wandering in the wilderness trusting God with which the children were blessed. The parents were really the children in things pertaining to God. The wilderness made the children the parents in the things pertaining to God.

The wilderness experience of the children prepared them to trust the Lord and obey Him. The circumstances had not changed, but the children had an experiential knowledge of a faithful God when faced with entering the Promised Land.

The children had time to develop a personal relationship with God in the wilderness while the parents really did not. The children, I believe had an advantage in faith, because they came to a personal knowledge of God and His faithfulness in the wilderness.

Yes, the parents saw miracles and experienced God's provision and discipline. But remember, they had 20 plus years as oppressed slaves and a few short years of God's presence in their lives. The children did not experience the worst of slavery and had 40 plus years of God's presence in their lives. The wilderness built a nation whose faith was in their faithful God.

Building faith in God takes time. Until the day we die and are with the Lord, we will need to be ever mindful of our need to grow in faith. We often forget that we will not meet with perfection here on earth. We will always fall short and need God to faithfully walk with us. God's goal is not that we won't need Him. God's goal is that we will wholly trust Him with our lives. God wants us to have faith in Him and His faithfulness.

CHAPTER 6

BIBLICAL TRUTHS

"And the people answered and said, "Far be it from us that we should forsake the Lord to serve other gods; for the Lord our God is He who brought us and our fathers up out of the land of Egypt, from the house of bondage, and who did these great signs in our sight and preserved us through all the way in which we went and among all the peoples through whose midst we passed."
Joshua 24:16, 17

The people of Israel said these words after conquering many of the inhabitants of the Promised Land while taking possession. They had experienced God's faithfulness in the wilderness and the fulfillment of His promises to Abraham, Isaac and Jacob of possessing the Promised Land. It is quite beautiful what they said.

God has provided their story to help us understand how He works in the lives of His children. He wants us to be able to say with them that He 'did these great signs in our sight and preserved us through all the way in which we went and among all the peoples through whose midst we passed.' In our day to day living, in our day to day struggling, we need to see God's faithfulness. We need to see Him in our midst. We need Him to preserve us in the world. We need Him to provide for us.

He wants us to find encouragement and hope from His faithfulness to them in their journey for our journeys as we learn to trust Him. While our wilderness experiences may vary, our God is the same. The biblical truths that applied to their wilderness experiences apply to ours.

Biblical Truth 1 – God Leads

God was the one leading the Israeli nation by day and night. He appeared as a cloud over the tent of meeting by day and as fire by night. They looked to God for their guidance in every detail of their lives. The nation did not move without God's leadership.

Jesus spoke of His leading in regards to His followers:

> *"But he who enters by the door is a shepherd of the sheep.*
> *To him the doorkeeper opens, and the sheep hear his voice,*
> *and he calls his own sheep by name, and leads them*
> *out. When he puts forth all his own, he goes before them,*
> *and the sheep follow him because they know his voice."*
> *John 10:2-4*

As believers, Jesus is our shepherd and we are His sheep. In these verses in John, Jesus is telling us that we will know His voice and will follow Him. I do not know anything about herding sheep, but I do know from what I have seen, the shepherd walks and the sheep faithfully follow. That is the picture Christ is portraying. Just as the sheep know the shepherd's voice and trustingly follow, we, as believers, know the Lord's voice and trustingly follow.

It takes time and trials to build this kind of trust in God's leadership that He wants in our relationship with Him. God wants to lead us 24 hours a day, 7 days a week, 52 weeks a year, for our entire lives. He wants to continually walk with us.

Biblical Truth 2 – God Disciplines Disobedience

When we looked at the wilderness journey of the Israelites, we read some passages that clearly spoke of God's discipline. God is committed to His work in our lives. Sometime do a word search of all the promises to those who fear the Lord. Fear of God's discipline is a healthy fear.

> *"The fear of the Lord is the beginning of wisdom;*
> *A good understanding have all those who do His*
> *commandments; His praise endures forever."*
> *Psalms 111:10*

Psalm 111:10 connects fear of the Lord with doing His commandments. God hates disobedience. God hates sin. How much does God hate it? Christ had to die on the cross to satisfy his hatred for it. Christ had to suffer both a physical and a spiritual death to satisfy the penalty for our sin. God is serious about the obedience of His children.

> *"My son, do not reject the discipline of the Lord, Or*
> *loathe His reproof, For whom the Lord loves He reproves,*
> *Even as a father, the son in whom he delights."*
> *Proverbs 3:11, 12*

I like how Proverbs 3:11, 12 states that it is because God loves us that he reproves us. God is not disciplining us out of judgment but out of love. The writer of Hebrews describes what God is accomplishing as He lovingly disciplines us:

> *"All discipline for the moment seems not to be joyful,*
> *but sorrowful; yet to those who have been trained by it,*
> *afterwards, it yields the peaceful fruit of righteousness."*
> *Hebrews 12:11*

God is training us in righteousness. The writer calls it peaceful fruit. Peaceful because it describes the relationship we have with God through Christ. Christ gives us peace; we are no longer enemies of our God.

Biblical Truth 3 – God Is Our Sole Provider

Have you ever considered that everything you have is the sole provision of the Lord? Everything! The job that provides the money to pay the bills is from God. Everything you have and will ever have is solely by the provision of God. For most of us, He has provided beyond just what we need, He has oversupplied us.

It may appear that people can have much without God providing and without them believing in His provision. However, what they have is also from God even if they do not believe it.

> *"...for He causes His sun to rise on the evil and the good,*
> *and sends rain on the righteous and the unrighteous."*
> *Matthew 5:45*

Matthew 5:45 addresses the most basic needs to sustain life; sun and water. Man needs God for His most basic needs. We would not have existence without God's provision. He doesn't need us to believe it for it to be true. That is the beauty of truth. It does not need to be believed to be true.

Listen to what Jesus says to Pilate:

> *"Pilate therefore said to Him, 'You do not speak*
> *to me? Do You not know that I have authority to*
> *release You, and I have authority to crucify You?'*
> *Jesus answered, 'You would have no authority over*
> *Me, unless it had been given you from above.'"*
> *John 19:10, 11*

Jesus made it known to Pilate that his authority did not come from men, but from God. Just because Pilate did not recognize it, did not make it so. As believers, we get to experience the truth of God's provision and grow in faith.

God does not need people to believe in Him for Him to provide on their behalf. God has chosen for us to know and experience the reality of His constant provision in our lives. It is a reason for rejoicing.

Knowing that God is the provider of all that we have is a special blessing. We are able to trust the Lord for provision and not stress or be anxious. There is peace in knowing God has provided and will continue to provide.

Biblical Truth 4 – God Prepares Us

I have really come to appreciate Christ's description of how He is with us in the preparing of us:

> *"Come to Me, all who are weary and heavy-laden,*
> *and I will give you rest. Take My yoke upon you,*
> *and learn from Me, for I am gentle and humble*
> *in heart; and you shall find rest for your souls.*
> *For My yoke is easy, and My load is light."*
> *Matthew 11:29, 30*

A yoke is the big cumbersome contraption that fits around the necks of oxen so they can work together. If someone had an inexperienced ox, he would yoke it with the more experienced ox, so that the more experienced could help teach the less experienced. I find it interesting that the yoke fits around the neck which supports the head where the mind resides.

Christ, the experienced one in things related to God wants to be yoked to us, the less experienced ones. He asks us to take His yoke upon us and learn from Him. He wants to teach us to become children of God who fully enjoy the promises and blessings of God our Father. Jesus, who is God, is willing to be yoked to us, sinners.

Christ assures us that He is gentle and humble in heart. When I think of someone who is gentle and humble in heart, I think of a very safe person. In other words, I do not need to fear.

By being yoked to us, Christ is committed to being with us. Because His yoke is easy and His load is light, we will find rest for our souls.

It is significant that we will find rest for our souls. When Adam and Eve sinned in the Garden of Eden, our souls lost their peace with their maker. Our souls no longer had rest in our relationship with God.

Ever since the eviction from the Garden, man has been trying to meet that need for peace and rest for his/her soul with other gods and things to believe in. However, that need can only be met in Christ. (In my book, *He Walks With Us*, I discuss a Saving Faith In Christ. I provide that important information in Appendix A to this book. Please read the information if you have not placed your faith in Christ.)

In the wilderness, God prepared the nation to worship only Him and depend only on Him. The wilderness prepared them to rest in Him in the Promised Land. Through our struggles in the wilderness, we learn to worship, trust and rest in God.

When you consider the hardships the Israeli nation encountered in the wilderness, you realize that it was not an easy life. God did make all the provision, but the Israeli nation endured pain and loss.

God walking with us does not mean that the hardships of life will not be present in our lives. God walking with us means that God is teaching us to live in His peace just as He taught the Israelites to live in His peace. The wilderness exercises our faith to understand God's faithfulness and to trust Him for our lives. Jesus tells us:

"Peace I leave with you; My peace I give to you:
not as the world gives, do I give to you. Let not
your heart be troubled, nor let it be fearful."
John 14:27

I do believe God is preparing us for work He planned for us. But, more importantly, I believe He wants us to have peace in our hearts in our relationship with Him. We find peace as we learn to trust Him in the wilderness.

CHAPTER 7

REFLECTION

*"On the glorious splendor of Thy majesty, And
on Thy wonderful works, I will meditate."*
Psalms 145:5

What an awesome privilege to glory in His majesty and meditate on
His wonderful works. When we are in the wilderness we get to see
His glory and His works. We see Him.

The Israelites saw Him continually leading them with the cloud.
Yes, God. The Israelites continually ate and drank of His provision
of manna and water. Yes, God. The Israelites continually experienced
victory in battle. Yes, God. The Israelites were continually disciplined.
That is hard to say, 'yes, God' to. My initial reaction was ouch.

All of God's works, including discipline, were necessary as I
reflect on the story of the Israeli nation. The children would never
have had the faith to enter the Promised Land had they not seen
God's glory and wonderful works in the wilderness.

To truly appreciate the work of the wilderness, we need only
consider the contrast of the two reports by the spies. The parents
report was:

> *"But the men who had gone up with him said, 'We*
> *are not able to go up against the people, for they*
> *are too strong for us....we became grasshoppers in*
> *our own sight, and so we were in their sight.'"*
> Numbers 13:31-33

The report of the children 40 years later was:

> *"And they said to Joshua, 'Surely the Lord has given*
> *all the land into our hands, and all the inhabitants*
> *of the land, moreover, have melted away before us."*
> Joshua 2:24

It is the same inhabitants. The difference is that the parents' eyes were focused on themselves; forty years later, the children's eyes were focused on God. The writer of Hebrews tell us:

> *"Therefore, since we have so great a cloud of*
> *witnesses surrounding us, let us also lay aside every*
> *encumbrance, and the sin which so easily entangles*
> *us, and let us run with endurance the race that*
> *is set before us, fixing our eyes on Jesus..."*
> Hebrews 12:1, 2

The verses tell us to fix our eyes on Jesus. In the wilderness, the children learned to fix their eyes on God. The children learned to look to God for the battles that lay ahead and that made the difference on how they viewed entering the Promised Land. As we fix our eyes on Jesus, it should make a difference in God's walk with us as we live in this world. The wilderness teaches us to fix our eyes on Jesus.

There is another difference between the parents and the children that I feel needs to be pointed out. It was the parents' fear that was really making the decision. They were afraid. Being afraid was not the problem, however. Their problem was their fear made the decision rather than faith in God.

Were the children afraid? I believe they were. Three times, in a mere five verses, before entering the Promised Land, God tells Joshua:

> *"Be strong and courageous...Only be strong*
> *and very courageous...Have I not commanded*
> *you? Be strong and courageous!"*
> *Joshua 1:5-9*

God asked Joshua to have courage. Joshua and the children must have had fear, if God asked Joshua to have courage. Notice that God did not say do not have fear. Joshua's feeling of fear was normal for the challenges the nation would be enduring. To encourage Joshua, God promised him:

> *"Just as I have been with Moses, I will be*
> *with you; I will not fail you or forsake you...*
> *Do not tremble or be dismayed, for the Lord*
> *your God is with you wherever you go."*
> *Joshua 1:5-9*

God assured Joshua that he could be strong and courageous because God would be with him just as He had been with Moses. God's faithfulness in Moses' life was a witness for Joshua's faith and the faith of the Israelites. God would be walking with them wherever He sent them just as He had been with Moses. God will be with us just as He was with Moses and Joshua. What a wonderful promise. Jesus tells us:

> *"and lo, I am with you always, even to the end of the age."*
> *Matthew 28:20*

Jesus promises us that He will always be with us. Through His Holy Spirit, He is with us; He will always be with us.

Finally, sandwiched between the encouragement to be strong and courageous and God's promise to be with Joshua is:

> *"be careful to do according to all the law which Moses*
> *My servant commanded you; do not turn from it to*
> *the right or to the left, so that you may have success*
> *wherever you go. This book of the law shall not depart*
> *from your mouth, but you shall meditate on it day and*
> *night, so that you may be careful to do according to*
> *all that is written in it; for then you will make your*
> *way prosperous, and then you will have success."*
> Joshua 1:5-9

Joshua is told to stay in the word of God and to meditate on it. Joshua would need the word of God to keep him strong in his faith in God. The Apostle Paul tells us:

> *"So faith comes from hearing, and*
> *hearing by the word of Christ."*
> Romans 10:17

It is reassuring to me that what God taught His children in the Old Testament, is the same as what He is teaching us in the New Testament. The word of God in our lives is necessary for our faith. We can learn from their lives.

Consider those areas in your life in which you are struggling. Can you see how the truths that God built into the nation of Israel are applicable to your situation?

Appreciating how God worked in the lives of those in the Bible helps us understand how He might be working in our lives. Just as He walked with the Israeli nation guiding their steps, He guides my steps. He guides your steps.

There are several verses that relate to what the Israeli nation learned that I often meditate on as I grow in my faith in God.

Jeremiah 29:11 (God has a plan as He leads):

> *"'For I know the plans that I have for you,'*
> *declares the Lord, 'plans for welfare and not for*
> *calamity to give you a future and a hope."*

Matthew 6:25-34 (God provides for us):

> *"For this reason I say to you, do not be anxious for your*
> *life, as to what you shall eat, or what you shall drink;*
> *nor for your body, as to what you shall put on. Is not*
> *life more than food, and the body than clothing? Look*
> *at the birds of the air, that they do not sow, neither do*
> *they reap, nor gather into barns, and yet your heavenly*
> *Father feeds them. Are you not worth much more than*
> *they? And which of you by being anxious can add a*
> *single cubit to his life's span? And why are you anxious*
> *about clothing? Observe how the lilies of the field grow;*
> *they do not toil or do they spin, yet I say to you that even*
> *Solomon in all his glory did not clothe himself like one of*
> *these. But, if God so arrays the grass of the field, which is*
> *alive today and tomorrow is thrown into the furnace, will*
> *He not much more do so for you, O men of little faith?*
> *Do not be anxious then, saying, 'What shall we eat?' or*
> *"What shall we drink?' or "With what shall we clothe*
> *ourselves?' For all these things the Gentiles eagerly seek;*
> *for your heavenly Father knows that you need all these*
> *things. But seek first His kingdom and His righteousness;*
> *and all these things shall be added to you. Therefore*
> *do not be anxious for tomorrow; for tomorrow will care*
> *for itself. Each day has enough trouble of its own."*

Ephesians 2:10 (God prepares us):

> *"For we are His workmanship, created in Christ*
> *Jesus for good works, which God prepared*
> *beforehand, that we should walk in them."*

Revelations 3:19 (God disciplines):

> *"Those whom I love, I reprove and discipline;*
> *be zealous therefore, and repent."*

God's word holds so much truth to help us on our journey. God is faithful to His word and to us. God wants so much more for us than we can even imagine. We need to learn to hope and trust.

God has a plan for you. God has a plan for me. Everything He allows in our lives is part of that plan. We may not always see how the pieces fit together, but God is fitting them together. We need to just trust and wait on Him. I am not saying it is easy, but it is worth it. God will be found faithful by us.

ABRAHAM

"By faith Abraham, when he was called, obeyed by going out to a place which he was to receive for an inheritance; and he went out, not knowing where he was going. By faith he lived as an alien in the land of promise, as in a foreign land, dwelling in tents with Isaac and Jacob, fellow heirs of the same promise; for he was looking for the city which has foundations, whose architect and builder is God. By faith even Sarah herself received ability to conceive, even beyond the proper time of life, since she considered Him faithful who had promised; therefore, also, there was born of one man, and him as good as dead at that, as many descendants as the stars of heaven in number, and innumerable as the sand which is by the seashore."
Hebrews 11:8-12

CHAPTER 8

STORY

"Now the Lord said to Abram, Go forth from your country, And from your relatives And from your father's house, To the land which I will show you; And I will make you a great nation, And I will bless you, And make your name great; And so you shall be a blessing; And I will bless those who bless you, And the one who curses you I will curse. And in you all the families of the earth shall be blessed."
Genesis 12:1-3

The first recorded communication between God and Abram (Abraham) is Genesis 12: 1-3. God told Abram to go forth to the land of Canaan; the land God promised that He would one day give to Abram's descendants. Abram was 75 years old. Sarai, his wife, was barren.

As commanded, Abram moved to Canaan as a sojourner. Abram's whole life was the life of a sojourner and so, there are many stories within his story. At first, it was actually hard to tell his story because he was always on the move. And then, I considered that we are all just sojourners as God's children? His story is our story.

Abram sojourned in Canaan until there was a famine in the land. Abram moved to Egypt to survive the famine. It is fascinating to see in Abram's life what would transpire in the life of his descendants. As we learned from the Israeli nation's story, it was a famine that led the nation to move to Egypt.

Fortunately for Abram, his stay was short. While in Egypt, though, he did have his faith in God tested concerning his true relationship to his wife, Sarai. God was faithful even though Abram was weak in faith.

Travelling with Abram this whole time was his nephew Lot and his family. If you have ever had extended family live with you, you can appreciate that it got a little crowded. Abram lets Lot choose where he will live and Abram will sojourn in the opposite direction. I like that it is in the opposite direction. I have felt that need.

Well, Lot was taken captive during a battle between warring kings and Abram needed to rescue him and his family. And while that story is interesting, I believe the two stories within that story are important messages of Abram's life.

The first of these two stories is that Abram tithed to Melchizedek after this victory in battle. The writer of Hebrews provides insight into who Melchizedek is:

> *"For this Melchizedek, king of Salem, priest of the Most High God, who met Abraham as he was returning from the slaughter of the kings and blessed him, to whom also Abraham apportioned a tenth part of all the spoils, was first of all, by the translation of his name, king of righteousness, and then also king of Salem, which is king of peace. Without father, without mother, without genealogy, having neither beginning of days nor end of life, but made like the Son of God, he abides a priest perpetually."*
> *Hebrews 7:1-3*

The writer of Hebrews continues with this declaration about Christ:

"For it is witnessed of Him, 'Thou art a priest
forever According to the order of Melchizedek.'"
Hebrews 7:17

I encourage you to read chapter 7 in the book of Hebrews. This encounter between Abram and Melchizedek is part of Abram's wilderness journey and part of Jesus' story. God had a reason for telling us this as part of Abram's journey. Melchizedek blessed Abram and Abram paid a tithe to this priest who was a symbol of Christ. Abram is the lesser of the two.

The second significant story is when Abram refused payment by a king of another city. This king wanted to pay Abram for waging the battle that rescued Lot. Genesis 14:23 tells us that Abram refused payment so that the king could not say that it was he who blessed Abram. I really have to ponder if I have allowed others to bless me and thus lost out on God's blessing? This story does make me give consideration when someone wants to somehow repay me for serving God.

Abram's tithe to Melchizedek was unto God. The payment from the king would not have been. Abram wanted others to know that all he had was the blessing of God.

God again made his covenant with Abram in Genesis 15:1. Abram honestly expressed his concern that he had no heir. God assured him that he would have an heir. He also forewarned Abram that his descendants must first incur enslavement and oppression for four hundred years. Abram would have an heir, but inheriting the Promised Land would be by future generations.

Realize that Abram was now 86 years old (11 years since the first promise from God) and his wife Sarai was barren. It appeared hopeless. Sarai was concerned that she had not given Abram his heir so she gave Abram her maid hoping for the heir. Ishmael was born by her maid Hagar. God's promise was that the heir would be by Sarai.

When Abram was 99 years old, God renewed His promise and commanded that Abram and all the males of the household be circumcised (Genesis 17). Circumcision would be a sign of the covenant between God and Abram and his descendants. Abram's name is changed to Abraham and Sarai's name to Sarah.

God had Abraham move again which created another opportunity for Abraham to exercise faith in God concerning his relationship to Sarah. Instead, Abraham gave into fear. None of us is perfect. God in His perfect faithfulness intervened.

Isaac, Abraham's heir, was finally born to Sarah. Abraham was now 100 years old. The years between God first giving Abraham the promise of an heir to the birth of the heir was 25 years.

There was great celebration over the birth of Isaac. Then, God tested the faith of Abraham by asking him to offer up his son, Isaac, as a sacrifice to the Lord. I love how the story shows Abraham exercising great faith in believing in the provision of God to provide a substitute sacrifice in his son's stead. God did provide a substitute sacrifice.

God's faithfulness endures forever. He provided His Son as a sin substitute sacrifice for us.

CHAPTER 9

WILDERNESS

"And Joshua said to all the people, 'Thus says the Lord, the God of Israel, 'From ancient times your fathers lived beyond the River, namely, Terah, the father of Abraham and the father of Nahor, and they served other gods.'"
Joshua 24:2

Joshua 24:2 gives us insight into Abraham's spiritual heritage. He was not raised to worship God. Sometimes we make assumptions about people's faith and we are wrong. We also often think God can't use us because of the weakness of our faith. God is the author and perfecter of our faith (Hebrews 12:2). He has a plan for us, just as He had a plan for Abraham. God chooses us just as we are, just as He chose Abraham.

Abraham's spiritual heritage did not keep God from choosing Abraham. In the wilderness, God built Abraham's faith in Him. God was faithful as Abraham grew in his faith. God shows the same faithfulness toward us as we grow in faith.

When I look at Abraham's wilderness life, I see four key tests of his faith. Three he failed. The critical fourth test he passed. I believe it was God's provision in his three failures as well as other wilderness experiences that led to his victory of faith in the fourth. I am encouraged by Abraham's story because I know that God will persevere in building my faith even when I fail.

Test 1 – Sarah Is My Sister

Here is the Biblical description of the opportunity afforded Abraham to exercise faith in God:

> *"And it came about when he came near to Egypt, that*
> *he said to Sarai his wife, 'See now, I know that you are*
> *a beautiful woman; and it will come about when the*
> *Egyptians see you, that they will say, 'This is his wife;'*
> *and they will kill me, but they will let you live. Please*
> *say that you are my sister so that it may go well with me*
> *because of you, and that I may live on account of you.'"*
> *Genesis 12:11-13*

Ironically, Abraham did not ask Sarah to tell a lie. Genesis 20:12 tells us that Sarah was Abraham's half-sister. They also weren't telling the truth. Abraham feared he would be killed if it was known they were married.

Abraham was faced with a choice. On the one hand, he has the promise of God to care for him and provide him with an heir. On the other hand, he is in a foreign land and knows the king in this land will look upon his wife with favor and most likely desire her which means his death. Does he allow his faith in God's promise or his fear for his life determine his choice?

Abraham chose to permit the fear for his life to dictate his decision. Rather than trust in the promise of God, Abraham hid behind Sarah and placed her in an improper situation for a wife. Abraham failed this test.

God faithfully intervened:

> *"But the Lord struck Pharaoh and his house with great*
> *plagues because of Sarai, Abram's wife. Then Pharaoh*
> *called Abram and said, 'What is this you have done to*
> *me? Why did you not tell me that she was your wife?*
> *Why did you say, 'She is my sister,' so that I took her for*
> *my wife? Now then, here is your wife, take her and go.'"*
> Genesis 12:17-19

Interestingly enough, Pharaoh feared God. His fear of God was greater than his desire for Sarah. He did not want to disobey God whom he did not worship.

Test 2 – The Birth of Ishmael

Sarah had not gotten pregnant. Remember, she was described as being barren. She encouraged Abraham to lay with her maidservant, Hagar, that they might have children through her. It was probably out of Sarah's understanding of the desire of her husband's heart for a descendant and her belief it would not be born of her that she made this offer. Sarah must have been enduring inner turmoil over her barrenness.

Abraham did have relations with Hagar and she bore him a son whom they named Ishmael. Ishmael by tradition is for the Arab nations what Jacob is for the Israeli nation. Ishmael had 12 sons (Genesis 25:12-18) from which became 12 tribes. These nations are actually brothers with the same father. Fascinating.

Abraham failed this test. God made a promise to him about his heir through Sarah. Rather than keeping his faith focused on the promise and helping Sarah stay faithful to the promise, he submitted to the opportunity for an heir afforded him by Sarah's maidservant. Abraham took matters into his own hands. Here is the Biblical story:

> *"Now Sarai, Abram's wife had borne him no children,*
> *and she had an Egyptian maid whose name was Hagar.*

> *So Sarai said to Abram, 'Now behold, the Lord has*
> *prevented me from bearing children. Please go in to*
> *my maid; perhaps I shall obtain children through her.'*
> *And Abram listened to the voice of Sarai. And after*
> *Abram had lived ten years in the land of Canaan,*
> *Abram's wife Sarai took Hagar the Egyptian, her*
> *maid, and gave her to her husband Abram as his*
> *wife. And he went in to Hagar, and she conceived."*
> *Genesis 16:1-4*

Notice that it says Abraham listened to the voice of Sarah. He was not listening to the voice of God. When we stop listening to God, it leads to sin for us. It led to sin for Abraham.

Test 3 – Sarah Is My Sister

Abraham gets a second chance to get this test right.

When I got a test back in college it was interesting the mixed feelings I had. I knew the ones I got wrong I would not get wrong again. The ones I got right I could not be as sure I would get right again. We learn from our mistakes.

Abraham did not learn from his mistake. Here is the Biblical story:

> *'Now Abraham journeyed from there toward the*
> *land of the Negev, and settled between Kadesh and*
> *Shur; then he sojourned in Gerar. And Abraham*
> *said of Sarah his wife, 'She is my sister.' So*
> *Abimelech king of Gerar sent and took Sarah."*
> *Genesis 20:1, 2*

The whole passage, Genesis 20:1-18, is a very powerful passage of God's intervention. Why did Abraham practice this bit of deception? He told Abimelech:

"I thought, surely there is no fear of God in this
place; and they will kill me because of my wife."
Genesis 20:11

Abraham's focus was on himself. He again allowed his fear to make his choice rather than have faith in God. He trusted his solution to the problem rather than trust God for a solution. Do you ever do that? I do. Too often I am coming up with my own solution to a problem while I am supposedly trusting God.

Abraham was not concerned with Sarah and what he was asking of her. He was not concerned with the danger in which he was placing Abimelech by allowing him to sin against God. When you read the whole passage you understand that God did not keep Abimelech from committing this sin against Sarah or Abraham. God said He prevented Abimelech from sinning against God.

Abraham miserably failed this test.

Test 4 – The Sacrifice Offering of Isaac

Isaac was finally born with much celebration. Then, we read:

"Now it came about after these things, that God tested
Abraham, and said to him, 'Abraham!' And he said,
'Here I am.' And He said, 'Take now your son, your
only son, whom you love, Isaac, and go to the land
of Moriah; and offer him there as a burnt offering
on one of the mountains of which I will tell you.'"
Genesis 22:1, 2

Abraham took Isaac and travelled as God had requested. When he got close to the place for the sacrifice:

> *"And Abraham said to his young men, 'Stay here*
> *with the donkey, and I and the lad will go yonder;*
> *and we will worship and return to you.'"*
> Genesis 22:5

Abraham was told to offer his son as a burnt offering and yet he told his servants that they would both return from worshipping the Lord. Abraham believed that God would provide. His faith in God's faithfulness had grown.

When they arrived where they would worship, Abraham proceeded with the process of offering up his only son as God asked of him. An angel of the Lord intervened:

> *"But the angel of the Lord called to him from*
> *heaven, and said, 'Abraham, Abraham!' And he*
> *said, 'Here I am.' And he said, 'Do not stretch out*
> *your hand against the lad, and do nothing to him;*
> *for now I know that you fear God, since you have*
> *not withheld your son, your only son, from Me.'"*
> Genesis 22:11, 12

The angel of the Lord also told Abraham:

> *"And in your seed all the nations of the earth shall*
> *be blessed, because you have obeyed My voice."*
> Genesis 22:18

Abraham believed he was to sacrifice his son. He also had faith that God would provide. I do not believe he knew how God would provide. Abraham by faith had to prepare to take his son's life without knowing. Let's read what the writer of Hebrews says:

> *"By faith Abraham, when he was tested, offered up*
> *Isaac; and he who had received the promises was*

offering up his only begotten son; it was he to whom it
was said, 'In Isaac your descendants shall be called.' He
considered that God is able to raise men even from the
dead; from which he also received him back as a type."
Hebrews 11:17-19

God chose to provide a ram as a substitute for the offering of Isaac. That is what our faithful God does. He provides sacrifices.

God provided Christ for us as a substitute for the penalty for our sins. Christ is the ultimate fulfillment of God's promise to Abraham to provide a sacrifice through which all the nations shall be blessed.

Abraham stepped out in faith and waited on God. We need to step out in faith and wait on God. Learning to wait on the Lord is part of the wilderness training. Fortunately, it is waiting on a faithful God.

Abraham passed the ultimate test.

CHAPTER 10

BIBLICAL TRUTHS

*"You see that faith was working with his works,
and as a result of the works, faith was perfected;
and the Scripture was fulfilled which says, "And
Abraham believed God, and it was reckoned to him as
righteousness," and he was called the friend of God."*
James 2:22, 23

Abraham learned to have faith in God in his wilderness experiences. Through the trials and tests, his faith was perfected and produced the works of God. It is said of him that "he was called the friend of God." His lessons of growing in faith are of value to us as faith is perfected in us.

Biblical Truth 1 – God is the Author and Fulfiller of His Promises

It was God who came to Abraham promising him an heir and that He would make him a great nation. It was God who promised to give Abraham's descendants the Promised Land. Abraham did not approach God. It was not a conditional promise on Abraham. God simply said what He would do.

Abraham did exercise faith by travelling to the Promise Land. God has us exercise faith through the course of fulfilling His promises. However, God is the author of His promises and fulfills His promises in His perfect time. God is also the author and perfecter of our faith (Hebrews 12:2).

I find great comfort that Abraham waited 25 years for the fulfilment of the promise of an heir. God was not in a hurry about the fulfillment of His promise. The promise was fulfilled in God's perfect time. God fulfills His promises toward me in His perfect time. When God has me wait, He isn't delaying in fulfilling His promise, He is accomplishing His work in me.

We need to be ever mindful that the promises belong to God and the fulfillment of the promises is with God on His schedule. Have you ever said, "But God, you promised?" Did God tell you the exact year, month, day, minute, second that He would fulfill His promise? God is not in a hurry. He is concerned with the faith He is building within us which takes time. His promises will be fulfilled.

Abraham was not the only person/nation affected by the promises or the timing of their fulfillment. This is what God told Abraham about the delay in the fulfillment of His promise that Abraham's descendants would inherit the Promised Land:

> *"And God said to Abram, 'Know for certain that your descendants will be strangers in a land that is not theirs, where they will be enslaved and oppressed four hundred years. But I will also judge the nation whom they will serve; and afterward they will come out with many possessions. And as for you, you shall go to your fathers in peace; you shall be buried at a good old age. Then in the fourth generation they shall return here, for the iniquity of the Amorite is not yet complete.'"*
> Genesis 15:13-16

"The iniquity of the Amorite is not yet complete." That is a powerful statement. God's promises don't just impact us. While our hope as Christians is to be in the center of God's will for us, we are not the center of His will. God will fulfill His promises concerning us in His perfect time according to His perfect will. The verse I claim as I wait upon the Lord is:

> *"Cease striving and know that I am God."*
> *Psalms 46:10*

Do not focus on the fulfillment of the promise. Focus on the Promise Maker. Our hope is in Him. What God has promised, He will perform.

Biblical Truth 2 – People Are Impacted By Our Poor Choices

Abraham's poor choice of saying Sarah was his sister impacted other people. A nation was vulnerable to suffering God's judgment for Abraham's choice. We will now look at other verses of the passage that involved Abimelech and his nation:

> *"Now Abimelech had not come near her; and he*
> *said, 'Lord, wilt Thou slay a nation, even though*
> *blameless? Did he not himself say to me, 'She is my*
> *sister'? And she herself said, "He is my brother.' In*
> *the integrity of my heart and the innocence of my*
> *hands I have done this.' Then God said to him in the*
> *dream, 'Yes, I know that in the integrity of your heart*
> *you have done this, and I also kept you from sinning*
> *against Me; therefore I did not let you touch her."*
> *Genesis 20:4-6*

Abraham did not exactly lie but he also did not tell the truth. His choice impacted Sarah, Abimelech and Abimelech's nation. Your choices impact those around you.

As I reflected on this truth this morning, the Lord gave me some insight into some of the struggles I have had in the work place. I was not someone who said what she thought people wanted to hear. I said what I thought should be said. I was careful with my words, but I would not say Sarah was my sister so I would not have to say she was my wife.

My struggle was with the fact that while I wanted that type of honesty in my relationship with my co-workers and bosses, they did not necessarily practice the same with me or each other. I wanted their support of me to be based on honesty and not my ability to manipulate the truth to my advantage. However, relationships in the workplace do not necessarily work that way. Our choices impact each other.

The verse that is always at the forefront of my mind and heart is:

"He who walks in integrity walks securely."
Proverbs 10:9

It is hard to walk in integrity. Little white lies are so tempting. Doesn't the end justify the means? Are you trusting your white lie or God? Abraham trusted his white lie. Yes, God intervened, but I don't think that is what He wants to have to do for His children. He wants our trust. Our hope should be that God intervenes as we walk uprightly, not as we choose our own solution first.

Biblical Truth 3 – People Are Impacted By Our Faith

Sometimes we think God's walk with us is in a vacuum. It isn't. People are watching our walks and are impacted by them. Abraham was not alone when he prepared to offer up Isaac as a sacrifice. Isaac was very much a participant in the act. He had the most at risk for his father's faith.

We always talk about Abraham when we talk about his willingness to sacrifice his son, but consider Isaac's role in this story. He was aware of what was happening. Dad says that they are going to make a sacrifice to the Lord and Isaac asks a poignant question:

> *"And Isaac spoke to Abraham his father and said,*
> *'My father!' And he said, 'Here I am, my son.'*
> *And he said, 'Behold, the fire and the wood, but*
> *where is the lamb for the burnt offering?'"*
> *Genesis 22:7*

Isaac had noticed that something was missing from this little journey, the sacrifice. It is important to have a lamb for the sacrifice, especially in the wilderness where there are no lambs. Abraham answers him:

> *"And Abraham said, 'God will provide for Himself*
> *the lamb for the burnt offering, my son.'"*
> *Genesis 22:8*

Isaac had faith in his father and faith in his father's faith. They walked on together. I have a feeling they were both lost in their feelings and thoughts as they walked on together.

They arrived and Abraham prepared to sacrifice his son:

> *"Then they came to the place of which God had told*
> *him; and Abraham built the altar there, and arranged*
> *the wood, and bound his son Isaac, and laid him on*
> *the altar on top of the wood. And Abraham stretched*
> *out his hand, and took the knife to slay his son."*
> *Genesis 22:9, 10*

Was this the same man who said Sarah was his sister? No, this was not the same man. Abraham prepared his son to be a sacrifice. While it is an amazing faith on the part of Abraham, it was Isaac who was tied, laying on top of the wood, with his father holding a knife ready to make him a sacrifice. Isaac was being impacted by Abraham's faith and his faith was also being tested.

God did what He does as a faithful God:

> *"Then Abraham raised his eyes and looked, and behold,*
> *behold him a ram caught in the thicket by his horns;*
> *and Abraham went and took the ram, and offered*
> *him up for a burnt offering in the place of his son."*
> *Genesis 22:13*

God provided a substitute sacrifice. Abraham was relieved. Isaac was relieved. This test of faith of Abraham was also a test of faith for Isaac.

When God tests our faith, others are impacted. Often their faith is supported by our faith, sometimes it is encouraged by our faith, and sometimes it is tested by our faith. We need to realize that our faith is not in a vacuum but is visible to those around us.

Do you consider the impact your faith has on others? It scares me to think my faith has an impact. The thought drives me to pray to God to sustain my faith.

CHAPTER 11

REFLECTION

"And he said, "Do not stretch out your hand
against the lad, and do nothing to him; for now
I know that you fear God, since you have not
withheld your son, your only son, from Me."
Genesis 22:12

As I reflect on Abraham's wilderness journey, the verse that I believe summarizes what God was doing in Abraham's life is Genesis 22:12. Abraham learned to fear God. I wonder if we discuss often enough that a healthy fear of God is good.

Ultimately, Abraham's story teaches us is to fear God first. Abraham's fear of God finally determined his choices. It wasn't a fear that had him cowering before God. It was a fear that made God's will the first and foremost desire of his heart.

Abraham offered up what was most important to the fulfillment of God's promises, his son. Abraham learned that God's relationship with Him was more important than anything else in his life. He was willing to sacrifice everything because of his devotion to God and God's relationship with him.

Listen to what Jesus said about our devotion to Him:

> *"If anyone comes to Me, and does not hate his own*
> *father and mother and wife and children and brothers*
> *and sisters, yes, and even his own life, he cannot*
> *be My disciple. Whoever does not carry his own*
> *cross and come after Me cannot be My disciple."*
> Luke 14:26, 27

God asked Abraham to come after Him first and foremost. God asked Abraham to leave all behind and follow Him. God is asking the same of us. When you think about carrying your cross, realize that that is what Christ did when He paid for our sins. He died on a cross. By carrying our cross, we are saying we will die to self, so we can live in Christ. That is what the Apostle Paul meant when he wrote:

> *"I have been crucified with Christ; and it is no longer*
> *I who live, but Christ lives in me; and the life which I*
> *now live in the flesh I live by faith in the Son of God,*
> *who loved me, and delivered Himself up for me."*
> Galatians 2:20

What is beautiful about God, is that when He asks something of us, He also provides a promise. Jesus is clear in His request in Luke 14:26 27, but He is equally clear in His promise:

> *"And everyone who has left houses or brothers*
> *or sisters or father or mother or children or farms*
> *for My name's sake, shall receive many times*
> *as much, and shall inherit eternal life."*
> Matthew 19:29

What a wonderful promise.

I do not think God literally expects us to leave everything. He desires a heart that would be willing too if He asked. God did not allow Abraham to sacrifice his son. He wanted Abraham to understand that God needed to be first in Abraham's life.

God requires hearts willing to sacrifice all for Him. Some have had to leave everything for their faith in God. History is full of believers who were persecuted for their faith. Even today, there are believers losing their lives for their faith. But for most of us, He is only asking for a willing heart.

I cannot say that I have fully learned this truth about a willing heart. I can say that I have experienced trusting God from a willing heart. And, I found God faithful even when I forgot.

My first goal in life was to work as an engineer at NASA. I wanted to be part of the space program. I chose my degree, Mechanical Engineering, and the university I attended with that one goal in mind.

I actually got to work at NASA as an engineer while I went to school. I would trade off semesters. It was an amazing experience.

In my final year in college, God asked me to forego being an engineer and working at NASA and become a missionary. I said yes to His calling. People constantly asked me why I would give up a promising engineering career to be a missionary. My answer was simple: God asked me to.

I always added to that answer that if God wanted me to be an engineer again someday that He would bring it to pass. Some twenty years later I was managing construction projects for a private university while obtaining my Master's degree in engineering management and my professional license in mechanical engineering. When I moved to Sacramento, I was hired as an engineer.

God has a plan for each of us. Nothing is lost by giving our lives over to the Lord. He is asking of us to have willing hearts.

God is the author of His promises and He fulfills His promises. His faithfulness is our hope.

We need to decide if He will be first in our lives. I like what Joshua says:

> *"...as for me and my house, we will serve the Lord."*
> *Joshua 24:15*

JACOB

"By faith Jacob, as he was dying, blessed each of the sons of Joseph, and worshipped, leaning on the top of his staff."
Hebrews 11:21

CHAPTER 12

STORY

"And the Lord said to her, 'Two nations are in your
womb; And two peoples shall be separated from
your body; And one people shall be stronger than
the other; And the older shall serve the younger.'"
Genesis 25:23

Isaac's wife, Rebekah, was pregnant with twins, Esau and Jacob. As they struggle in her womb, God describes to Rebekah in Genesis 25:23 the future relationship of her two sons and their subsequent nations; "The older shall serve the younger."

Esau was the older. Jacob was the younger. Isaac loved Esau. Rebekah loved Jacob. God chose Jacob. God chose Jacob before he was born. God chose us before we were born.

I can only imagine the competitiveness between Jacob and Esau because of the obvious affections of the parents. We actually see it played out when Esau sold his birthright to Jacob for the instant gratification of food. Esau knew Jacob would want a price for the food Jacob had. Jacob would not share out of brotherly love. Esau was willing to pay it and gave up his birthright. Jacob had the advantage because he had what Esau wanted.

If having Esau's birthright was not enough, later, with his mother's help, Jacob obtained Esau's blessing from his father as well (Genesis 27:1-29). Jacob now had Esau's birthright and his blessing. Esau was understandably angry towards Jacob. Actually, he bore a grudge:

> *"So Esau bore a grudge against Jacob because of the blessing with which his father had blessed him; and Esau said to himself, 'The days of mourning for my father are near; then I will kill my brother Jacob.'"*
> Genesis 27:41

Bearing a grudge implies a deep, long felt emotion. As we can see by Esau's words, he was willing to kill his brother to satisfy his grudge. How sad.

These words of Esau were made known to Rebekah and she was worried. She encouraged Jacob to flee from Esau to her family for a few days.

On his journey to his mother's family, Jacob had his own vision (Genesis 28:12-15) in which God made the promise to Jacob that He made to Abraham concerning a nation of descendants. Rebekah's plan for the journey was for Jacob to flee Esau for a few days. God's plan for Jacob's journey was to build Jacob's faith in God.

I wonder what Jacob was expecting when he arrived at the home of Laban, his mother's brother. He had his vision. He was his mother's favorite son. Did he expect a hero's welcome? Have you ever expected people to be excited about your presence only to be disappointed? I have. I think Jacob was.

Whatever he felt, it was forgotten when he met Laban's younger daughter, Rachel. Jacob fell in love with Rachel. He made a deal with Laban to work for seven years for Rachel's hand in marriage. His few days journey would last at least seven years.

When the seven years ended, Laban gave Jacob his older daughter, Leah, in marriage, not Rachel. Jacob had been tricked.

Jacob had to agree to another seven years of labor for Rachel's hand in marriage.

Obviously, with Jacob having wives, he started having kids and wanted to go home. Laban, however, had prospered and did not want Jacob to leave. It is actually quite interesting what Laban says to Jacob:

> *"But Laban said to him, 'If now it pleases*
> *you, stay with me; I have divined that the*
> *Lord has blessed me on your account.'"*
> Genesis 30:27

Jacob and Laban made another deal. Jacob continued to manage Laban's herds but all spotted, black and otherwise less desirable of the flock would belong to Jacob as his wages.

Jacob wisely planned the mating of the flocks so that his herd increased while Laban's herd decreased. Laban and his sons are upset that Jacob's flock prospered while their flock suffered. It is interesting that they were upset that Jacob was benefitting from his own labors. They did not mind when they benefitted from his labors. But now that he is benefitting, they are upset. Ever experience that in the workplace?

After six years of Jacob's flock increasing, God told Jacob to return to his home. Fearing the worse from Laban and his sons, Jacob, his family and his livestock left without telling Laban.

When Laban learned that Jacob had fled, he pursued Jacob. God warned Laban in a dream not to speak good or bad of Jacob. Laban heeded the warning. It might seem reasonable that Laban heeded the warning, but Laban was not a worshipper of God. We learn that when he asks for his gods back which Rachel had stolen (Genesis 31:30). It is interesting how people can have a fear of God whom they do not believe in.

After the encounter with Laban, Jacob continued his journey home. He actually sent everyone ahead of him, so he could wrestle with the Lord in prayer. Jacob did not know what awaited him and wanted to be sure of God's blessing. As a result of the wrestling, his name was changed to Israel (Genesis 32:24-30).

After wrestling with the Lord, with humility in his heart and faith in the Lord, here is his response to his brother Esau:

> *"And Jacob said, 'No, please, if now I have found*
> *favor in your sight, then take my present from my*
> *hand, for I see your face as one sees the face of*
> *God, and you have received me favorably. Please*
> *take my gift which has been brought to you, because*
> *God has dealt graciously with me, and because I*
> *have plenty.' Thus he urged him and he took it."*
> *Genesis 33:10, 11*

Jacob is welcomed home by his brother. The Bible does not tell us Esau's story, but obviously, God was working in his heart as well.

CHAPTER 13

WILDERNESS

*"And he had a dream, and behold, a ladder was set on
the earth with its top reaching to heaven; and behold,
the angels of God were ascending and descending on
it. And behold, the Lord stood above it and said, 'I
am the Lord, the God of your father Abraham and the
God of Isaac; the land on which you lie, I will give it to
you and to your descendants. Your descendants shall
also be like the dust of the earth, and you shall spread
out to the west and to the east and to the north and to
the south; and in you and in your descendants shall
all the families of the earth be blessed. And behold, I
am with you, and will keep you wherever you go, and
will bring you back to this land; for I will not leave
you until I have done what I have promised you.'"*
Genesis 28:12-15

Jacob had the vision in Genesis 28:12-15 at the beginning of his
wilderness journey as he fled his brother, Esau. I find it interesting
how God gives some of His children (Abraham, Jacob, Joseph, and

David to name a few) a vision of how He would use them prior to their wilderness journeys.

God does not always give us their verbal response, but He does give us Jacob's. I admire Jacob's response:

> *"Then Jacob made a vow, saying, 'If God will be with me*
> *and will keep me on this journey that I take, and will give*
> *me food to eat and garments to wear, and I return to my*
> *father's house in safety, then the Lord will be my God.'"*
> *Genesis 28:20, 21*

Doesn't Jacob's response in Genesis 28:20, 21 say what we feel? God, if you do this, I will believe. Does not our faith require God's faithfulness? Jacob knew he needed God for his journey. We need God for our journeys. Our faith needs God's faithfulness.

With God's promise on his mind, I believe Jacob, as his mother's favorite son, expected to be treated fairly and kindly by his Uncle Laban. Here is Jacob's description of his treatment in his uncle's home:

> *"These twenty years I have been in your house; I served*
> *you fourteen years for your two daughters, and six*
> *years for your flock, and you changed my wages ten*
> *times. If the God of my father, the God of Abraham,*
> *and the fear of Isaac, had not been for me, surely*
> *now you would have sent me away empty-handed."*
> *Genesis 31:41, 42*

Those verses do not provide a description of being treated fairly and kindly. In fact, Jacob uses the word affliction to describe his time in the wilderness serving Laban. However, Jacob also acknowledges that God had been with him. Jacob found God faithful as he asked in Genesis 28. Jacob's Uncle Laban may not have kept his promises, but God kept His.

I have often wondered why Jacob kept serving his uncle Laban if he was so deceitful in his treatment of Jacob. Why didn't Jacob just leave and return home? Surely his parents could provide gifts to compensate Laban for his daughters.

I believe Jacob did not leave because as he saw God's faithfulness, he submitted to His leading. Jacob did not leave until God said to leave:

> *"Then the Lord said to Jacob, 'Return to the land of your fathers and to your relatives, and I will be with you.'"*
> *Genesis 31:3*

Notice that when God tells Jacob to return, He also tells him that he will be with him. Jacob is not alone in his journey. We are not alone in our journeys. God is with us and will always be with us.

We are not given a lot of detail about Jacob's wilderness time with Laban, but we do know a few things: It was not easy. Laban changed his wages ten times. Jacob worked basically 24/7. God blessed Laban while Jacob labored. Jacob did not leave until God told him to.

We also know that God fulfilled Jacob's request in Genesis 28:20, 21 such that Jacob came to his own faith in the God of his fathers. Jacob's wilderness journey was not easy, but it was successful. Jacob saw the faithfulness of God in his life and he grew in his faith in God.

CHAPTER 14

BIBLICAL TRUTHS

"But regarding the fact that the dead rise again, have you not read in the book of Moses, in the passage about the burning bush, how God spoke to him, saying, 'I am the God of Abraham, and the God of Isaac, and the God of Jacob'? He is not the God of the dead, but of the living; you are greatly mistaken."
Mark 12:26, 27

Jacob went from believing because of his fathers, to believing because he had a personal relationship with God. I like how Mark 12:26, 27 says it: God is the God of Abraham, Isaac and Jacob. God is the God of Jacob forever. In Christ, God is our God for eternity. What a wonderful blessing.

When I study Jacob's wilderness journey, I see two biblical truths that contributed to Jacob's growth in faith in God. While there is much to his life that is worth studying, these are the truths that have helped me the most in my struggles.

Biblical Truth 1 – God is Personally Involved with Us

God wants a personal relationship with us. As Mark 12:26, 27 depicts, God identifies Himself as the God of people with names. He knows His chosen personally. He also wants to be known personally by His chosen. What an honor to know God and be known by Him.

Jacob's personal journey with God began with a promise just as Abraham's did. I am glad Jacob's journey begins with the promise of God. It demonstrates God's faithfulness to His promise to Abraham across generations. It also demonstrates His commitment to Jacob as the heir of the promise.

Jacob's response to his promise in Genesis 28:20, 21 accurately depicts why I believe we need a wilderness journey in God's personal walk with us. It is in the wilderness that we find God faithful in His personal care for us just as the Israeli nation, Abraham and Jacob did. The wilderness takes God from being a God others believe in, to a faithful God we believe in. His walk with us becomes a personal walk.

Listen to what Jacob says on his journey home, after serving Laban:

> *"I am unworthy of all the lovingkindness and of all the faithfulness which Thou hast shown to Thy servant;"*
> *Genesis 32:10*

Jacob in Genesis 32:10 is acknowledging that God had answered his prayer in Genesis 28: 20, 21. Jacob understood that all that God did since his journey began was because of God's choice of him. He experienced God faithfully involved in his life. And, Jacob was humbled by the knowledge. When we realize how much God has done on our behalf, it humbles us. We are unworthy. In Christ, we are made worthy.

It is encouraging that Jacob could say that about God because his 'employment' by Laban was difficult. Laban was not honest with Jacob. Laban tricked Jacob and changed his wages. Yet, Jacob persevered in his service as unto God. Jacob viewed God as in control and trusted God through it. It could not have been easy to trust God day after day as Laban dealt treacherously with him.

I have been in jobs where I have wanted to quit because of unfair treatment. I have experienced the broken promises and the changed wages. But like Jacob, I also knew God's faithfulness and His unwavering blessing on me.

God has a bigger plan for us than the situation we are in. God is concerned with our growth in faith in Him. God is concerned with who we are becoming. When I think about what God was doing in Jacob's life and will do in our lives, I think of what the writer of Hebrews says:

> *"It is for discipline that you endure; God deals with you as with sons; for what son is there whom his father does not discipline? But if you are without discipline, of which all have become partakers, then you are illegitimate children and not sons. Furthermore, we had earthly fathers to discipline us, and we respected them; shall we not much rather be subject to the Father of spirits, and live? For they disciplined us for a short time as seemed best to them, but He disciplines us for our good, that we may share His holiness. All discipline for the moment seems not to be joyful, but sorrowful; yet to those who have been trained by it, afterwards it yields the peaceful fruit of righteousness."*
> *Hebrews 12:7-11*

The phrase in these verses that stands out for me is, 'who have been trained by it.' I instantly think of soldiers going through boot camp training. The soldiers are receiving disciplined training that will hopefully keep them alive if they find themselves in a battle during war.

The wilderness is like boot camp training. Jacob was growing in the 'peaceful fruit of righteousness' while laboring for Laban. We see the peaceful fruit of righteousness in his communication when he saw his brother again. Jacob left home an arrogant boy and returned a humble man.

As we find ourselves in those difficult situations, like Jacob, we need to be mindful of God's personal involvement in our lives. God's plan is our righteousness. His plan is our eternal salvation. God is committed to our good. He is personally involved.

Biblical Truth 2 – Wrestle in Prayer

After fleeing Laban and before being reconciled to Esau, Jacob prayed many times. I want to focus on this prayer experience:

> *"Then Jacob was left alone, and a man wrestled with*
> *him until daybreak...And he blessed him there."*
> Genesis 32:24-29

After his wilderness journey, Jacob had the confidence to wrestle in prayer with God. Jacob wanted his blessing from God and he got it. His wrestling with God reminds me of a parable on prayer that Jesus told:

> *"Now He was telling them a parable to show that at all*
> *times they ought to pray and not to lose heart, saying,*
> *'There was in a certain city a judge who did not fear*
> *God, and did not respect man. And there was a widow*
> *in that city, and she kept coming to him, saying, 'Give me*
> *legal protection from my opponent.' And for a while he*
> *was unwilling; but afterward he said to himself, 'Even*
> *though I do not fear God nor respect man, yet because this*
> *widow bothers me, I will give her legal protection, lest by*
> *continually coming she wear me out.'' And the Lord said,*
> *'Hear what the unrighteous judge said; now shall not God*
> *bring about justice for His elect, who cry to Him day and*

*night, and will He delay long over them? I tell you that He
will bring about justice for them speedily. However, when
the Son of Man comes, will He find faith on the earth?"*
Luke 18:1-8

When it comes to praying God's promises, like Jacob, like the widow, we should be relentless in our prayers. Jacob wrestled with God because of the promise God had made concerning his descendants. He feared facing Esau and wanted God's assurance of His blessing.

Wrestling in prayer takes effort. The perseverance of the widow required a faithful commitment to time and action. She refused to give up. Often, I think we give up too soon. We need to be willing to be committed to prayer to our God.

Jacob's prayer life changed in the wilderness. God became the God he hoped in. He wanted nothing more than God's blessing on his life. He has grown in his prayer life and in God's walk with him.

I want nothing more than God's blessing on my life. I don't know if I wrestle enough in prayer. And since I am asking the question, I guess I am not. I do know that I pray that I will become a prayer warrior. I want to be someone who will go to battle in prayer for myself and others.

CHAPTER 15

REFLECTION

*"All these are the twelve tribes of Israel, and this is what
their father said to them when he blessed them. He blessed
them, every one with the blessing appropriate to him.
Then he charged them and said to them, "I am about
to be gathered to my people; bury me with my fathers
in the cave that is in the field of Ephron the Hittite,
in the cave that is in the field of Machpelah, which is
before Mamre, in the land of Canaan, which Abraham
bought along with the field from Ephron the Hittite for
a burial site. There they buried Abraham and his wife
Sarah, there they buried Isaac and his wife Rebekah,
and there I buried Leah - the field and the cave that
is in it, purchased from the sons of Heth." When Jacob
finished charging his sons, he drew his feet into the bed
and breathed his last, and was gathered to his people."*
Genesis 49:28-33

In Genesis 49, Jacob on his death bed let his sons know that he did
not want to be buried in Egypt. He wanted to be buried with his

family in the land promised his descendants. Jacob was still looking forward to the promise.

As I reflect on Jacob's life, I see a man whose knowledge of God became very personal. God went from being the God of Jacob's fathers, to Jacob's faithful God. I also see a young, arrogant boy who became a humble servant of God. Jacob changed.

This change is most apparent when I compare Jacob's relationship with his brother before his wilderness journey to the man he became who encountered his brother at the end. It is obvious that Jacob is not the boy who fled twenty years earlier. He was changed in the wilderness. The wilderness should change us.

Jacob's wilderness journey began because he was fleeing his brother. His journey ended by being reconciled to his brother. What a beautiful picture.

Prior to his wilderness journey, Jacob and his brother did not have the best relationship. As Jacob is returning home, Genesis 32:11 tells us that he feared Esau. This is how Jacob approached Esau:

> *"But he himself passed on ahead of them*
> *and bowed down to the ground seven times,*
> *until he came near to his brother."*
> *Genesis 33:3*

And,

> *"...for I see your face as one sees the face of God..."*
> *Genesis 33:10*

Despite his fear, Jacob humbled himself before his brother. Personally, I think Jacob knew he deserved his brother's wrath for his treachery. He experienced treachery while working for Laban.

Despite his fear, Jacob acknowledged his brother. Jacob gave worth to his brother. Jacob valued his brother. Jacob did not cower. With courage, he bowed to his brother. What a tender act of love.

Before the wilderness, getting his brother's birthright and blessing was Jacob's claim. Upon returning, God's blessing was his strength. Those twenty years of waiting on the Lord while he labored for his Uncle Laban changed Jacob. He had God's blessing and he knew that it was enough.

Jacob had God's acknowledgment and so, he could acknowledge his brother. God acknowledges us. God wants us to acknowledge others. We give worth and value to people when we acknowledge them.

Have you ever considered the effect you have on someone by acknowledging them? It is very powerful. Jacob's acknowledgment of his brother was powerful. Jacob could acknowledge his brother because he knew he had God's blessing on his life. God's blessings on our lives should impact our relationships with others.

Before I leave Jacob's story, I want to also reflect on his faithfulness in his laboring for Laban. His faithfulness has a message to us who are in difficult employment situations.

It would have been easy for Jacob to get discouraged. His uncle wasn't being honest with him. He was working long hours for someone else's benefit. He was barely able to provide for his family. Basically, his uncle was taking advantage of him.

Jacob easily could have quit. But, he didn't. He trusted God and God provided. After all his labors for Laban, Jacob was able to say that all that he had was a result of God's blessing on his life. He understood that God was in control of his circumstances. Hear what he said:

> *"...the God of my father has been with me...."*
> *Genesis 31:5*

In the midst of a difficult situation, Jacob recognized that God was with him. He was able to see God in his circumstances. He understood that he labored for God and not for Laban.

Do we see God in our circumstances? Do we see God in our workplace? Do we wait on the faithfulness of God?

We need to trust God, like Jacob, for the circumstances in which we find ourselves. We need to look past our circumstances and trust God. God will be faithful to us.

JOSEPH

*"By faith Joseph, when he was dying, made
mention of the exodus of the sons of Israel,
and gave orders concerning his bones."*
Hebrews 11; 22

CHAPTER 16

STORY

"And he said to them, 'Please listen to this dream which I have had; for behold, we were binding sheaves in the field, and lo, my sheaf rose up and also stood erect; and behold, your sheaves gathered around and bowed down to my sheaf.' Then his brothers said to him, 'Are you actually going to reign over us? Or are you really going to rule over us?' So they hated him even more for his dreams and for his words. Now he had still another dream, and related it to his brothers, and said, 'Lo, I have had still another dream; and behold, the sun and the moon and eleven stars were bowing down to me.' And he related it to his father and to his brothers; and his father rebuked him and said to him, 'What is this dream that you have had? Shall I and your mother and your brothers actually come to bow ourselves down before you to the ground?" And his brothers were jealous of him, but his father kept the saying in mind."
Genesis 37:6-11

Joseph was the first son born to Rachel but the eleventh son born to Jacob (Israel). His story begins in Genesis 37 at the age of 17. Jacob loved Joseph more than all his other sons which created problems between him and his brothers (sound similar to Jacob and Esau).

Joseph like his father was given visions from God (Genesis 37:6-11). He shared the visions with his father and brothers. These visions only added to his brothers' jealousy and hatred toward him.

One day, while his brothers were tending the flock, Jacob sent Joseph to obtain news as to how the brothers and the flock were doing. The brothers saw him from a distance and to satisfy their hatred, planned his death. Reuben prevented his death, but was absent when they sold him into slavery. His brothers slayed an animal and covered Joseph's multicolored tunic, given to him by their father, with the blood to convince Jacob that Joseph was dead.

Joseph became a slave in the house of Potiphar. Potiphar recognized that God blessed everything that Joseph did. Thus, Potiphar placed Joseph as overseer over everything he owned including his home (Genesis 39:4).

Potiphar's wife also took an interest in Joseph. She found him attractive and wanted him to lay with her. The Bible says that she desired him. Joseph refused.

Potiphar's wife's flirted day after day until one day she grabbed ahold of his tunic. When Joseph fled, she still held his tunic. She falsely accused Joseph of trying to take advantage of her to Potiphar. Joseph was thrown into prison.

God blessed Joseph in jail. The chief jailer recognized the blessing of God upon Joseph and put him in charge of everything concerning the jail.

The Pharaoh's chief cupbearer and baker were also thrown in prison and met Joseph. They had dreams which Joseph interpreted. His interpretation of their dreams told them that they would be released in three days. Joseph asked them to remember him.

You notice how God likes three days. In three days the chief cupbearer and baker will leave the dungeons of prison and enter into the Pharaoh's presence. One will live (chief cupbearer) and one will die (chief baker). Did the chief cupbearer remember Joseph? Not immediately.

It was two years before the chief cupbearer remembered Joseph. The Pharaoh had a dream that no one could interpret. The cupbearer told the Pharaoh about Joseph's ability to interpret dreams and so, the Pharaoh requested Joseph. Joseph interpreted the dream.

The dream told Pharaoh that there would be seven years of abundance followed by seven years of famine. Joseph encouraged Pharaoh to find someone wise to manage the years of abundance to prepare for the years of famine. The Pharaoh selected Joseph.

The famine impacted Jacob and his family. He sent his sons to Egypt to buy grain. They bowed before Joseph and requested to purchase grain. What was Joseph's dream? His brothers would bow down before him.

Joseph recognized his brothers but they did not recognize him. Joseph revealed himself to his brothers and they were reconciled. Jacob and the whole family moved to Egypt and were cared for by Joseph.

CHAPTER 17

WILDERNESS

*"And the Lord was with Joseph, so he
became a successful man."*
Genesis 39:2

What an amazing statement. 'The Lord was with Joseph, so he became a successful man.' Do you realize that the Lord is with you? It is an overwhelming thought that I will be successful simply because the Lord is with me. The Lord is committed to our success. Do you fathom that you will be successful because the Lord is with you?

Joseph was successful in three critical life situations in his wilderness journey that are valuable lessons for God's walk with us. He was a slave. He fled active temptation. He was a prisoner. Joseph's time as a slave and prisoner expanded 13 years. How Joseph handled his life situations in his wilderness journey is a witness for us.

He Was a Slave

Joseph was a slave. Someone owned him. His life is very different from his visions of his family bowing down to him. Joseph is bowing down to another.

He was faithful as a slave, though. He was faithful to God. This is the impact it had on Potiphar, an Egyptian:

> *"Now his master saw that the Lord was with him and how the Lord caused all that he did to prosper in his hand. So Joseph found favor in his sight, and became his personal servant; and he made him overseer over his house, and all that he owned he put in his charge. And it came about that from the time he made him overseer in his house, and over all that he owned, the Lord blessed the Egyptian's house on account of Joseph; thus the Lord's blessing was upon all that he owned, in the house and in the field. So he left everything he owned in Joseph's charge; and with him there he did not concern himself with anything except the food which he ate."*
> *Genesis 39:3-6*

Joseph may have been a slave, but more importantly, he was a servant of God being prepared for God's purpose. He faithfully served his master, Potiphar, as he served the Lord. We are servants of God being prepared for His purpose.

Joseph was learning to manage another man's property for that man's profit. Joseph received no wages. He was a slave. Yet, he faithfully managed everything concerning Potiphar's property.

Isn't this what his job for Pharaoh required? Wasn't he managing Egypt's abundance of grain for the profit of the Pharaoh?

We are not told if Joseph grumbled or complained about his situation. We are told that this favorite son of a rich father served as a slave honorably. Joseph is a testimony of serving the Lord faithfully in a difficult employment situation.

He Fled Active Temptation

Genesis 39:7 tells us that Potiphar's wife 'looked with desire at Joseph.' She wanted Joseph to lie with her and told him so. Joseph responded:

> *"But he refused and said to his master's wife, 'Behold,*
> *with me here, my master does not concern himself*
> *with anything in the house, and he has put all that*
> *he owns in my charge. There is no one greater in*
> *this house then I, and he has withheld nothing from*
> *me except you, because you are his wife. How then*
> *could I do this great evil, and sin against God?'"*
> *Genesis 39:8-9*

Joseph first talked about the great honor her husband had bestowed upon him by trusting him with everything. Joseph was a slave and spoke of feeling honored. Have you ever felt honored when a co-worker or boss or someone else profited from your work?

Joseph was given more responsibility because it benefitted his master. Joseph was not given his freedom as a reward or wages as a valued employee, just more responsibility. Joseph considered it an honor to be given more responsibility.

He then said that this act which she desired would be a great evil and a sin against God. He could have left it at a great evil. However, the real issue for Joseph was that it would be a sin against God. He did not say sin against Potiphar which it would have been. The compelling reason for his refusal was that it would be a sin against God. Not just a sin, but a sin against God.

She did not give up; she actively pursued Joseph. Genesis 39:10 tells us that 'she spoke to Joseph day after day.' She was persistent.

Along comes a day when no other man is about the house. Do you get the feeling she is setting one final trap to seduce Joseph? Here is what happened:

> *"And she caught him by his garment, saying,*
> *'Lie with me!' And he left his garment in*
> *her hand and fled, and went outside.'*
> Genesis 39:12

Joseph did not try to reason with her this time. He did not talk with her. He ran. He knew the dangerous situation he was in.

The Bible does not tell us if he truly was tempted or not. The Bible tells us that what Potiphar's wife wanted him to do he considered sin against God and so he fled. Joseph did not give sin a chance to take root in his heart, and thus become something he would act on. Joseph was focused on being faithful to His faithful God.

He Was a Prisoner

What did Joseph get for choosing not to sin with Potiphar's wife? He got thrown into prison. Doesn't seem fair. Joseph did nothing wrong. Actually, he did something very right. And what happened as of a result of his right behavior? Joseph's situation got worse; he got thrown in prison.

Joseph, however, continued to serve the Lord in spite of his circumstances:

> *"But the Lord was with Joseph and extended kindness*
> *to him, and gave him favor in the sight of the chief*
> *jailer. And the chief jailer committed to Joseph's*
> *charge all the prisoners who were in the jail; so that*
> *whatever was done there, he was responsible for it.*
> *The chief jailer did not supervise anything under*

> *Joseph's charge because the Lord was with him; and*
> *whatever he did, the Lord made to prosper."*
> Genesis 39:21-23

Joseph did not have a pity party. He did not blame God for his circumstances. He remained faithful where God had him. The chief jailer, like Potiphar, noticed that Joseph was blessed and entrusted the care of the jail to him. The chief jailer knew he was a servant of the Lord that could be trusted.

Joseph accepted where God had him and he faithfully served. He did not struggle with the unfairness of his situation. He trusted God. He trusted God's purpose. What might have been God's purpose for Joseph's prison time?

In prison, Joseph learned to manage desperate people in a desperate situation. What did he do for Pharaoh? He managed a desperate situation, the famine. He managed desperate people.

Was God preparing Joseph for his ultimate purpose? Yes. Joseph was faithful with the lessons. Joseph trusted in the faithfulness of God concerning him.

Often the trials we endure are preparing us for God's purpose for our lives. James encourages us to:

> *"Consider it all joy, my brethren, when you*
> *encounter various trials, knowing that the*
> *testing of your faith produces endurance. And let*
> *endurance have its perfect result, that you may*
> *be perfect and complete, lacking in nothing."*
> James 1:2-4

I find it interesting that both Potiphar and the chief jailer saw that God blessed Joseph. They did not personally believe in God and yet saw God's hand in Joseph's life. Do unbelievers see Him working in our lives? Do we trust in God's faithfulness for our lives?

CHAPTER 18

BIBLICAL TRUTHS

*"So then, my beloved, just as you have always obeyed, not
as in my presence only, but now much more in my absence,
work out your salvation with fear and trembling; for it
is God who is at work in you, both to will and to work
for His good pleasure. Do all things without grumbling
or disputing; that you may prove yourselves to be
blameless and innocent, children of God above reproach
in the midst of a crooked and perverse generation,
among whom you appear as lights in the world."*
Philippians 2:12-15

Joseph's faith exemplifies Philippians 2:12-15. He was a light as
a slave, as a prisoner and as Pharaoh's servant. I admire Joseph's
steadfast faithfulness to God. Joseph is my best friend as far as
biblical characters are concerned.

There are three main biblical truths I gain from the life
experiences of Joseph. God has used these truths over and over in
my life, especially in the workplace.

Biblical Truth 1 – Faithfulness Where God Has Us

Joseph was faithful as a slave, faithful as a prisoner, faithful as Pharaoh's servant. Joseph considered his service as unto the Lord wherever the Lord placed him. I think it is important to realize that Joseph saw his service as unto the Lord. In the final analysis, God was his master, not Potiphar, not the chief jailer, and not the Pharaoh.

The verses that come to mind are:

> *"And if you have not been faithful in the use of that which*
> *is another's, who will give you that which is your own?*
> *No servant can serve two masters; for either he will hate*
> *the one, and love the other, or else he will hold to one, and*
> *despise the other. You cannot serve God and mammon."*
> *Luke 16:12-13*

Joseph's life is a testimony of these verses. He was faithful in managing Potiphar's property. He was faithful in managing the jail. When the Pharaoh trusted him to manage the grain for the famine, he was faithful. His faithfulness, however, was to his one master, God.

Yes, Potiphar owned his body, but God owned his heart. His relationship with God is why he could say to Potiphar's wife that it would be sin against God. God was his master.

Yes, his body was in prison. But his heart freely loved the Lord and served the Lord.

Yes, he was Pharaoh's right hand man. However, in his heart, it was for the Lord's purpose that he managed the grain through the famine. He accomplished God's will not the will of Pharaoh.

When God is our master, we will be faithful regardless of our circumstances. Our circumstances are not our master, God is our master.

We need to remember that ultimately we work for God and not others and not for bosses. God is our Master. This is a difficult principle when we are in the circumstance. We need to fix our eyes on Jesus and not the circumstance.

Biblical Truth 2 – Forgiveness of Others

When Joseph's brothers came to him to buy grain he recognized them. They, however, did not recognize him. Genesis 42:1-9 tells the story.

Joseph decided to test them because he was concerned for his younger brother Benjamin. He actually told his brothers that as a test, they would not be allowed to leave unless the younger brother comes. He threw them into prison for three days. There is that three days again.

Here is what the brothers say about the test:

> *"Then they said to one another, 'Truly we are guilty concerning our brother, because we saw the distress of his soul when he pleaded with us, yet we would not listen; therefore this distress has come upon us.' And Reuben answered them, saying, 'Did I not tell you, 'Do not sin against the boy'; and you would not listen? Now comes the reckoning for his blood'"*
> Genesis 42:21-22

Joseph heard these words and wept. Finally, Simeon stayed and the other brothers left. Eventually, the other brothers returned with Benjamin.

When he saw Benjamin, Joseph revealed himself to his brothers and said:

> *"And now do not be grieved or angry with*
> *yourselves, because you sold me here; for God*
> *sent me before you to preserve life."*
> *Genesis 45:5*

Joseph forgave them. His forgiveness was based on his understanding of God's plan for his life. He accepted that what happened was all part of God's plan for him. He understood Biblical Truth 3 (below).

Our forgiveness of others is important to God. God actually ties our experience of His forgiveness to our ability to forgive others (Matthew 6:12). We need to extend forgiveness to others in order to grow in God's walk with us. It is not always easy, but it is imperative for God's walk with us.

Biblical Truth 3 – God Works All Things Toward our Good

Three times, in a short passage, Joseph told his brothers that it was God that sent him to Egypt ahead of them:

> *"Then Joseph said to his brothers, 'Please come closer*
> *to me.' And they came closer. And he said, 'I am your*
> *brother Joseph, whom you sold into Egypt. And now*
> *do not be grieved or angry with yourselves, because you*
> *sold me here; for God sent me before you to preserve*
> *life. For the famine has been in the land these two*
> *years, and there are still five years in which there will*
> *be neither plowing nor harvesting. And God sent me*
> *before you to preserve for you a remnant in the earth,*
> *and to keep you alive by a great deliverance. Now,*
> *therefore, it was not you who sent me here, but God."*
> *Genesis 45:4-8*

Joseph recognized the hand of God in His life. He understood that God allowed the slavery and the prison time to prepare him to preserve the life of his family. The Apostle Paul tells us:

> *"And we know that God causes all things to work*
> *together for good to those who love God, to those*
> *who are called according to His purpose."*
> *Romans 8:28*

Joseph's story is living proof that God works all things 'for good to those who love Him.' Joseph submitted to God's wilderness journey for him and God used Joseph to preserve the tribe of Israel. Joseph is a wonderful example of God orchestrating the experiences of the life of one of His children to accomplish His purpose.

As I look back at my journey, I can see experiences that prepared me for other experiences. God was always in control. It did not always feel like it when I was in the situation but, when I look back I can see His faithfulness in my life.

CHAPTER 19

REFLECTION

"I came that they might have life, and
might have it abundantly."
John 10:10

One of the reasons I like the story of Joseph so much is because, in spite of his life seemingly going in the wrong direction, Joseph was faithful to God. He did not let his circumstances define him. God's relationship with him defined him. Joseph had every reason to be discouraged and yet he served faithfully and waited on the Lord.

We talk about the abundant life (John 10:10) as if our lives will only be full of God's blessings. And believe me, the Christian life is full of God's blessings. What we really mean, though, is that only good things happen to us if we are trusting God.

If I look at the life of Joseph, I see that life can get worse before it gets better. He went from being the favorite son to being a slave to being a prisoner. Was that an abundant life?

If we asked Joseph he would say yes because God was with him. For Joseph, God was the abundant life. Christ said:

"I am the way, and the truth, and the life; no
one comes to the Father, but through Me."
John 14:6

The same Greek word for life is used in both John 10:10 and John 14:6. What kind of life has Jesus given believers? He has given us His life. He has given us eternal life. I believe the abundant life is a full spiritual life lived by faith in Christ through the power of the Holy Spirit. Joseph's life teaches us that he did, too.

For Joseph, God was in control of his life and he experienced God's presence in his life. He was able to say to his brothers that it was God who caused everything that happened in his life. He was fully aware of God working in and through him. His experience of God was the abundant life.

Do we experience God as the abundant life? Are we content that our relationship to God through Christ is the abundant life? I am learning this slowly but surely.

Do we recognize God at work in our circumstances or do we blame others? Joseph did not blame others.

Do we do the right thing and have circumstances get worse? Joseph fled Potiphar's wife only to find himself in prison.

Do we stay faithful to God even when life seems unfair? Joseph stayed faithful. He was faithful in the house of Potiphar and in jail. He was entrusted with everything by those who ruled over him.

Do we help people expecting them to help us and then get upset when they forget? Joseph interpreted the dreams of the chief cupbearer and chief jailer and was forgotten for two years. He was not remembered until the need for the Pharaoh's dream to be interpreted.

Joseph is an example of someone who trusted the Lord in spite of his circumstances. He accepted the events in his life as being part of God's plan for his life. He forgave those who injured him. He could forgive them because he knew God in a very personal way.

After Jacob died, Joseph's brothers are concerned that he might seek revenge and so, ask forgiveness. It is his brothers only recorded request for forgiveness. They only make the request because they believe that their father is no longer a shield for them. Joseph's response is a wonderful example for us all to remember:

> *"But Joseph said to them, "Do not be afraid, for am I*
> *in God's place? And as for you, you meant evil against*
> *me, but God meant it for good in order to bring about*
> *this present result, to preserve many people alive."*
> Genesis 50:19, 20

Yes, Joseph's life was impacted because of the sin of his brothers. Yet, He was able to accept it from the hand of God. He could see God's faithfulness in his circumstances and forgive.

Joseph's life story encourages me to stay faithful. Joseph's life story encourages me to forgive. God allows things in my life to build me for the future. I heard a speaker once say that God is preparing us for life's toughest moments. The moment we are in is not it.

Joseph's life is a witness to us that God uses our experiences to prepare us for His purpose. Joseph's experiences prepared him to be used by God to preserve the Israeli nation. Our experiences prepare us for God's purpose for us. The Apostle Paul tells us:

> *"For we are His workmanship, created in Christ*
> *Jesus for good works, which God prepared*
> *beforehand, that we should walk in them."*
> Ephesians 2:10

Joseph walked in the good works God prepared beforehand for him. He was faithful as a slave, as a prisoner, and finally as Pharaoh's steward. He had an abundant life in his relationship with God.

God did bless his life. As Pharaoh's right hand man he lived in luxury. But, even then, I think Joseph would say his abundance was the Lord's relationship with him.

Life can be difficult, but like Joseph we need to stay faithful to God. He is working out the plan He has for us. Life sometimes may not make sense to us, but God is in control. Our big problem in our small world, is a small problem in God's big world. We need to live by faith in a faithful God.

OTHER WITNESSES

*Now faith is the assurance of things hoped
for, the conviction of things not seen. For by
it the men of old gained approval."*
Hebrews 11:1, 2

CHAPTER 20

MOSES

"By faith Moses, when he was born, was hidden for
three months by his parents, because they saw he was a
beautiful child; and they were not afraid of the king's
edict. By faith Moses, when he had grown up, refused
to be called the son of Pharaoh's daughter; choosing
rather to endure ill-treatment with the people of God,
than to enjoy the passing pleasures of sin; considering
the reproach of Christ greater riches than the treasures
of Egypt; for he was looking to the reward. By faith
he left Egypt, not fearing the wrath of the king; for he
endured, as seeing Him who is unseen. By faith he kept
the Passover and the sprinkling of the blood, so that he
who destroyed the first born might not touch them."
Hebrews 11:23-28

Moses spent 82 years in the wilderness. He spent 40 years as part of
his journey and 42 more years with the nation of Israel. At the end of
the 82 years he did not enter the Promised Land. Numbers 20:1-13
tells the story of how Moses' journey ended. We will read verses 7-12:

> *"and the Lord spoke to Moses, saying, 'Take the rod; and*
> *you and your brother Aaron assemble the congregation*
> *and speak to the rock before their eyes, that it may yield*
> *its water. You shall thus bring forth water for them out*
> *of the rock and let the congregation and their beasts*
> *drink.' So Moses took the rod from before the Lord, just*
> *as He had commanded him; and Moses and Aaron*
> *gathered the assembly before the rock. And he said to*
> *them, 'Listen now, you rebels; shall we bring forth water*
> *for you out of this rock?' Then Moses lifted up his hand*
> *and struck the rock twice with his rod; and water came*
> *forth abundantly, and the congregation and their beasts*
> *drank. But the Lord said to Moses and Aaron, 'Because*
> *you have not believed Me, to treat Me as holy in the*
> *sight of the sons of Israel, therefore you shall not bring*
> *this assembly into the land which I have given them.'"*
> *Numbers 20:7-12*

Ever think a sin is a little sin? After everything Moses has endured with this people (including 40 years in the wilderness for their lack of faith), defending them to the Lord on numerous occasions, he finally acted out in anger. I am surprised it took him this long.

Moses's acting out his anger, however, was a sin against God. The act of sin was not the anger, it was the striking of the rock. God told Moses to speak to the rock. Moses was frustrated with their grumbling and so, rather than speak to the rock, he striked the rock.

It seems like a little sin. In God's world, no sin is little. He tells Moses that he did not treat Him as holy. Ouch. Do you ever think of your sin as treating God as unholy? That is not a little thing. God was not upset with Moses for being angry. God was upset with Moses because his action of anger was dishonoring to God.

Disobedience is disobedience regardless of the individual. Moses would not enter the Promised Land because of his sin. God did not have a different rule for Moses than the people of the nation. Joshua will lead the people into the Promised Land.

Moses situation hits where it hurts. Sin is serious to God. We say it all the time and yet I am not sure we fully grasp it. When I consider Moses, it is real. From my point of view, if anyone deserved to enter the Promised Land it was Moses. From God's point of view, Moses was no more deserving than anyone else.

Sin is an equalizer of people. We are all sinners. As Christians, we are forgiven and will not pay the penalty for our sin (Christ paid the penalty). We may, however, suffer consequences.

The consequences can be significant. Moses not entering the Promised Land was significant. He would die in the wilderness with those who did not believe God and with those who worshipped other gods. His position did not save him.

I know God's way is the right way. I know God's way is the perfect way. I still feel bad for Moses. Moses, however, accepted God's verdict and continued to faithfully serve. He faithfully prepared Joshua.

Moses has come a long way from the burning bush (Exodus 3:1-4:17). Moses was not a confident leader when God first chose him. He actually requested that God pick someone else. God chose Moses. Moses became a faithful servant of God.

The only sin of Moses mentioned, is this fatal sin. This fatal sin, however, was before the nation. Moses was a representative of God and He misrepresented God. The consequence for misrepresenting God was that he would not enter the Promised Land.

As Christians, we are representatives of God. What a huge responsibility. Fortunately, we have been given the Holy Spirit by which to live out this responsibility. Jesus told His disciples:

> *"But you shall receive power when the Holy Spirit has
> come upon you; and you shall be My witnesses..."*
> Acts 1:8

There is that word witnesses again. Just like the cloud of witnesses, like Moses, are our witnesses, we are witnesses to other believers and unbelievers. We testify of God's forgiveness and faithfulness in our lives.

It is an amazing thought that we are witnesses of God's faithfulness and forgiveness. We are members of the cloud of witnesses for others. I am not saying we deserve to be. I am saying we are.

My hope, through the Holy Spirit, is that Christ's life in and through me will be deserving. I look to God's word to teach me. I look to the lives of other members of the cloud to teach me. I trust the Holy Spirit within me to keep me.

CHAPTER 21

JONATHAN

"Greater love has no one than this, that
one lay down his life for his friends."
John 15:13

I admire Jonathan. While he is not mentioned in Hebrews 11, he was a man of faith, he is a witness of faith for me. Out of love, he was willing to lay down his life for David.

Saul, his father, was the king of Israel and Jonathan was heir to the throne. Jonathan understood, though, that God had taken the throne from the family of Saul and given it to the family of David. He supported God's choice, David.

Jonathan believed in the plan of God over the plan of man. He believed that who God anointed was the heir to the throne, not who his father anointed. He was a man of faith in God. Jonathan's faith is worth studying.

It is shortly after David slays Goliath that David is presented to Saul. Jonathan is immediately David's friend and supporter:

"Now it came about when he had finished speaking
to Saul, that the soul of Jonathan was knit to the

> soul of David, and Jonathan loved him as himself.
> And Saul took him that day and did not let him
> return to this father's house. Then Jonathan made
> a covenant with David because he loved him as
> himself. And Jonathan stripped himself of the robe
> that was on him and gave it to David, with his armor,
> including his sword and his bow and his belt."
> 1 Samuel 18:1-4

Jonathan swore allegiance to David and then gives David everything that identified Jonathan as heir to the throne. Jonathan was acknowledging David as heir to the throne. I am just so impressed.

I have been considered along with others for a promotion and I can tell you that I was not so cordial. Resentment or jealousy would be words I might use. Jonathan graciously supported God's choice. I needed to see the selection as God's choice. Jonathan helped me with the lesson.

Jonathan was not resentful or jealous. He made a covenant with David and clothed David. That is faith in God. He wanted what God wanted.

Jonathan protected David from his father, King Saul, on several occasions. I want to look at the story in 1 Samuel 20 when David asks why Saul is seeking his life. Jonathan does not believe his father is, but agrees to investigate. They arrange a meeting time and sign:

> "When you have stayed for three days, you shall go down
> quickly and come to the place where you hid yourself on
> that eventful day, and you shall remain by the stone Ezel."
> 1 Samuel 20:19

There is that three days again. 1 Samuel 20 also records a covenant between David and Jonathan:

> *"And if I am still alive, will you not show me the*
> *lovingkindness of the Lord, that I may not die? And*
> *you shall not cut off your lovingkindness from my house*
> *forever, not even when the Lord cuts off every one of*
> *the enemies of David from the face of the earth."*
> 1 Samuel 20:14, 15

Before I say more:

> *"Then Saul's anger burned against Jonathan and he said*
> *to him, "You son of a perverse, rebellious woman! Do I*
> *not know that you are choosing the son of Jesse to your*
> *own shame and to the shame of your mother's nakedness?*
> *For as long as the son of Jesse lives on the earth, neither*
> *you nor your kingdom will be established. Therefore now,*
> *send and bring him to me, for he must surely die.""*
> 1 Samuel 20:30-31

David is the son of Jesse.

Both Saul and Jonathan realized that either Jonathan or David must die. David must die for Jonathan to be king. Jonathan must die for David to be king. Saul knows that Jonathan has chosen death that David may be king.

Jonathan has accepted his fate. Here is what is sad to me, Jonathan won't be king, not because of any sin he has committed, but because of the sin of his father. Jonathan is a good man. Jonathan is a man of God. He is also the son of Saul and will share in his father's judgment.

Sin is damaging in our lives and the lives of those around us. Jonathan sets the example as to how we should respond. He submitted to God's judgment and supported God's choice.

Jonathan and Saul died in battle. This is what David said when he lamented Jonathan's death:

> *"How have the mighty fallen in the midst of the battle! Jonathan is slain on your high places. I am distressed for you, my brother Jonathan; You have been very pleasant to me. Your love to me was more wonderful Than the love of women. How have the mighty fallen, And the weapons of war perished!"*
> *2 Samuel 1:25-27*

David lost a friend in Jonathan. A friend who willingly submitted to God's plan for him and David.

Jonathan had choices. Jonathan could have helped his father in his attempts to kill David, he could have stayed neutral, or he could help David. He chose to help David.

Actually, He chose to be obedient to God's choice. He chose to serve God in His plan for David. He definitely is a witness to me of being faithful to God.

I feel the pings of jealousy when someone gets to do what I want to do. I sometimes wonder why them and not me. I am learning to pray for their success. I am learning to thank them for the work they are doing. I am learning to set aside that sin that so easily entangles me.

I am learning to do as Jonathan did. He set aside his claim to the throne for God's chosen one. He put God's will first and not his own.

CHAPTER 22

DANIEL, SHADRACH, MESHACH AND ABEDNEGO

*"And what more shall I say? For time will fail me
if I tell of Gideon, Barak, Samson, Jephthah, of
David and Samuel and the prophets, who by faith
conquered kingdoms, performed acts of righteousness,
obtained promises, shut the mouths of lions,
quenched the power of fire, escaped the edge of the
sword, from weakness were made strong, became
mighty in war, put foreign armies to flight."*
Hebrews 11:32-34

Daniel shut the mouths of lions and Shadrach, Meshach and Abednego quenched the power of fire. Their stories are intertwined in the book of Daniel, though Daniel is the main character.

The four of them were taken into captivity by Nebuchadnezzar, king of Babylon. They were selected to be officials in the king's court. Typically, when a male was selected to be an official in the king's court, he became a eunuch. Suffice to say, becoming a eunuch meant the inability to participate in the consummation of a marriage. Their devotion would be to the king only.

These four young men, however, had a higher devotion than the king. They were devoted to the God of Israel. They served Him before they served the king.

This devotion shows up early in their training when they request to only be served vegetables and water. They did not want to eat the meat because the animal probably had been sacrificed to false gods. The Israelites were not permitted to eat meat sacrificed to pagan gods. God grants them favor in the eye of the commander and they prosper without eating the meat.

They eventually rise to favor, especially Daniel. Daniel, like Joseph, is an interpreter of dreams. After Daniel interpreted the dream, that no one else could:

> *"Then King Nebuchadnezzar fell on his face and did homage to Daniel, and gave orders to present to him an offering and fragrant incense. The king answered Daniel and said, 'Surely your God is a God of gods and a Lord of kings and a revealer of mysteries, since you have been able to reveal this mystery.' Then the king promoted Daniel and gave him many great gifts, and he made him ruler over the whole province of Babylon and chief prefect over all the wise men of Babylon. And Daniel made request of the king, and he appointed Shadrach, Meshach and Abednego over the administration of the province of Babylon, while Daniel was at the king's court."*
> Daniel 2:46-49

These four men rose to prominence in the king's court. However, they also stayed true to God. They did not allow the security of their positions to weaken their faith.

Their faith is soon tested. Nebuchadnezzar made a gold image and required everyone to bow done before it. Meshach, Shadrach, and Abednego do not bow down before it and charges are brought against them before Nebuchadnezzar. They understood that the penalty for disobeying would be to be thrown into a fiery furnace. In other words, be burned alive.

Nebuchadnezzar gave them another chance to bow down to the image he made but they refused. I admire their response:

> *"If it be so, our God whom we serve is able to deliver us*
> *from the furnace of blazing fire; and He will deliver us*
> *out of your hand, O king. But even if He does not, let it be*
> *known to you, O king, that we are not going to serve your*
> *gods or worship the golden image that you have set up."*
> Daniel 3:17-18

They stepped into the furnace knowing God could save them but not knowing if he would. From the story, they did not appear to fear the fire. That is faith. God has asked less of me and I don't believe I have exercised that kind of faith. I would like that kind of faith.

They should have burned up immediately. However, when Nebuchadnezzar looks into the furnace there are four men walking around. He wanted this fourth man identified; many believe it was the Lord. When the three exited, Nebuchadnezzar was so impressed with their God he issued an edict that no one was to speak against the God of Israel.

God delivered them and it had a profound impact on the king and the nation. Do we avoid confrontations and miss out on opportunities for God to have a profound impact on those around us? I wonder. No one likes confrontation. Yet, because of these men facing the confrontation, God was able to do a great deliverance.

I do not know why Daniel was not included in the above story, because I am sure he also did not bow down. He did get his opportunity later though when his enemies came up with a plan. The story is told in Daniel 6. Here was what his enemies said:

> *"Then these men said, 'We shall not find any ground*
> *of accusation against this Daniel unless we find*
> *it against him regard to the law of his God.'"*
> *Daniel 6:5*

Daniel's service to the King was impeccable. They could find no fault with him. So, they resorted to treachery in regard to Daniel's devotion to God. I can't think of a higher honor from men. The plan required Daniel to make a choice of faith:

> *"All the commissioners of the kingdom, the prefects*
> *and the satraps, the high officials and the governors*
> *have consulted together that the king should establish*
> *a statute and enforce an injunction that anyone who*
> *makes a petition to any god or man besides you, O*
> *king, for thirty days, shall be cast into the lions' den."*
> *Daniel 6:7*

Enticed by the flattery and not considering the consequences, the king signed the document. Daniel's choice:

> *"Now when Daniel knew that the document was signed,*
> *he entered his house (now in his roof chamber he had*
> *windows open toward Jerusalem); and he continued*
> *kneeling on his knees three times a day, praying and giving*
> *thanks before his God, as he had been doing previously."*
> *Daniel 6:10*

Daniel continued his ritual of bowing down in prayer to God. His enemies caught him, as was the plan, and reported him to the king. The king had no choice but to throw him into the lion's den. However:

> *"Then the king went off to his palace and spent the*
> *night fasting, and no entertainment was brought*
> *before him; and his sleep fled from him."*
> Daniel 6:18

The king cared about Daniel and hoped that Daniel's God would deliver him. God did deliver Daniel. King Darius' responded to Daniel's deliverance by glorifying God:

> *"I make a decree that in all the dominion of my kingdom*
> *men are to fear and tremble before the God of Daniel;*
> *For He is the living God and enduring forever, And His*
> *kingdom is one which will not be destroyed, And His*
> *dominion will be forever. He delivers and rescues and*
> *performs signs and wonders In heaven and on earth, Who*
> *has also delivered Daniel from the power of the lions."*
> Daniel 6:26, 27

I am humbled by the faith of Daniel, Meshach, Shadrach and Abednego. They stood firm in their faith in God, in spite of the danger they would face in doing so. The danger was actually death. God faithfully delivered them.

As I reflect on their choices, I can think of how easy it would have been for Meshach, Shadrach and Abednego to say that while they bowed their bodies out of respect of the king, they did not bow their hearts. Daniel could say that while I won't bow my body to God out of respect to the king, I will continue to bow my heart. Or, Daniel could have closed the curtains and hidden what he was doing. Those options sound good. For them it was not a choice.

I am glad it was not a choice for them. People would have seen the physical action or inaction, not their hearts. If Meshach,

Shadrach and Abednego had bowed, it would have seemed that their fear of the furnace was greater than their faith in their God. If Daniel had not bowed to pray or had closed the curtains, it would seem that his fear of the lions was greater than his faith in his God.

People are watching us. They are observing if our actions are consistent with our faith. These four young men passed the test; their actions were consistent with their faith. I daresay that that is not always true of me.

I have at times stood firm in my faith. I also at times, have not. Fortunately, God loves me through those times and continues to teach me. Abraham is a great reminder that God builds our faith and stays faithful even when we don't have faith. These four men are a wonderful example of faith in the midst of trials.

I find the contrast between the two scenarios faced by these four men fascinating. The three could bow their bodies and not their hearts, while Daniel could bow his heart and not his body. The three were to pay homage to the king's statue and Daniel was not to pay homage to his God.

For all four it was basically death to stand firm in their faith. They stood firm and God was honored. God was honored because of their faith. I want my faith to honor God.

CHAPTER 23

PAUL

"For you have heard of my former manner of life in Judaism, how I used to persecute the church of God beyond measure, and tried to destroy it; and I was advancing in Judaism beyond many of my contemporaries among my countrymen, being more extremely zealous for my ancestral traditions. But when He who had set me apart, even from my mother's womb, and called me through His grace, was pleased to reveal His Son in me, that I might preach Him among the Gentiles, I did not immediately consult with flesh and blood, nor did I go up to Jerusalem to those who were apostles before me; but I went away to Arabia, and returned once more to Damascus Then three years later I went up to Jerusalem to become acquainted with Cephas, and stayed with him fifteen days."
Galatians 1:13-18

I have not always appreciated the Apostle Paul. It is only as I have grown in my understanding of Romans 7 and 8 that I have grown to appreciate this man of faith. Paul shared his faith with us. He shared his humanness with us. He shared his walk with God with us.

Paul actually begins his story as Saul in Acts 7:58 at the stoning of Stephen:

> *"And Saul was in hearty agreement with putting him to death. And on that day a great persecution arose against the church in Jerusalem;...But Saul began ravaging the church, entering house after house; and dragging off men and women, he would put them in prison.""*
> Acts 8:1-3

As Saul, Paul was a strong persecutor of early Christians:

> *"Now Saul, still breathing threats and murder against the disciples of the Lord, went to the high priest, and asked for letters from him to the synagogues at Damascus, so that if he found any belonging to the Way, both men and women, he might bring them bound to Jerusalem."*
> Acts 9:1, 2

Paul willingly persecuted Christians. It was a mission for him. On the way to Damascus, however, Saul meets Jesus:

> *"And it came about that as he journeyed, he was approaching Damascus, and suddenly a light from heaven flashed around him; and he fell to the ground, and heard a voice saying to him, "Saul, Saul, why are you persecuting Me?" And he said, "Who art Thou, Lord?" And He said, "I am Jesus whom you are persecuting,""*
> Act 9:3-5

Saul is blinded by the light and is led by the hand to Damascus. For three days he waits for another message from the Lord. There is that three days again. Ananias, as directed by the Lord, comes to Saul:

> *"And Ananias departed and entered the house, and*
> *after laying his hands on him said, "Brother Saul,*
> *the Lord Jesus, who appeared to you on the road by*
> *which you were coming, has sent me so that you may*
> *regain your sight, and be filled with the Holy Spirit"...*
> *and immediately he began to proclaim Jesus in the*
> *synagogues, saying, "He is the Son of God.""*
> Acts 9:17-20

Saul, who was persecuting believers, is now a believer. This created a bit of chaos for the church and he is sent off to Tarsus. Several years pass before his story is picked up again in Acts 11 with Barnabas seeking him out.

When we read Acts, it is not obvious that years have passed between when Saul fled to Tarsus and Barnabas finds him again, but it makes sense. Saul was a Pharisee and received strict teaching of the scriptures. That strict teaching prepared him to argue as to how Jesus could not be the promised Messiah. Now, he believes in Jesus. God will now teach Him to argue that Christ is the promised Messiah.

It is in Acts 13 that he now becomes known to us as Paul and he is sent on his first missionary journey. Paul has started his apostolic ministry. I have read that thirteen years passed between Paul's conversion and his first missionary journey.

It is amazing to think that God used a leading persecutor of the church to be one of the church's boldest ambassadors. Paul who was present and approved of the stoning of Stephen is now a brother in Christ's family. God chooses His children and He chose Paul.

What I admire about Paul is his devotion to God. As a Pharisee, his zeal was out of a devotion to God. When Christ revealed himself to Paul, his devotion was to Christ who is God. Paul was not devoted to his religion and that set him apart as a Pharisee. His devotion was to God.

As a Pharisee, his understanding of the scriptures had been skewed by his teachers. As Christ taught him, his knowledge became the basis of what we study to understand God's plan for us in Christ.

God's plan is that we have a personal relationship with Him through Christ. Christ paid the penalty for our sins so we could have a personal relationship with God. What amazing knowledge!

Paul describes that relationship and the Christian's challenges, struggles and most importantly, hope. He lived it. He suffered it. He was victorious in faith.

Paul wrote 13 of the 24 New Testament books. Some feel he wrote Hebrews as well. Because of the use of Old Testament scriptures in Hebrews, it is logical to assume Paul wrote it.

When I think about what Paul learned most during his wilderness journey (the thirteen years between his salvation and first apostolic ministry), I think of:

> *"although I myself might have confidence even in the flesh. If anyone else has a mind to put confidence in the flesh, I far more: circumcised the eighth day, of the nation of Israel, of the tribe of Benjamin, a Hebrew of Hebrews; as to the Law, a Pharisee; as to zeal, a persecutor of the church; as to the righteousness which is in the Law, found blameless. But whatever things were gain to me, those things I have counted as loss for the sake of Christ. More than that, I count all things to be loss in view of the surpassing value of knowing Christ Jesus my Lord, for whom I have suffered the loss of all things, and count them but rubbish in order that I may gain Christ, and may be found in Him, not having a righteousness of my own derived from the Law, but that which is through faith in Christ, the righteousness which comes from God on the basis of faith, that I may know*

Him, and the power of His resurrection and the fellowship
of His sufferings, being conformed to His death; in order
that I may attain to the resurrection from the dead."
Philippians 3:4-11

In man's eyes, Paul was a man of God on his own merit. In
God's eyes, Paul needed Christ. Paul learned that he needed Christ.
We need Christ. And what was Paul's abundant Christian life like:

"Are they servants of Christ? (I speak as if insane) I
more so; in far more labors, in far more imprisonments,
beaten times without number, often in danger of death.
Five times I received from the Jews thirty-nine lashes.
Three times I was beaten with rods, once I was stoned,
three times I was shipwrecked, a night and a day I have
spent in the deep. I have been on frequent journeys, in
dangers from rivers, dangers from robbers, dangers from
my countrymen, dangers from the Gentiles, dangers
in the city, dangers in the wilderness, dangers on the
sea, dangers among false brethren; I have been in labor
and hardship, through many sleepless nights, in hunger
and thirst, often without food, in cold and exposure."
2 Corinthians 11:23-27

Out of fairness to Paul, here is how he described his abundant
life:

"I know how to get along with humble means,
and I also know how to live in prosperity; in
any and every circumstance I have learned the
secret of being filled and going hungry, both of
having abundance and suffering need. I can do
all things through Him who strengthens me."
Philippians 4:12, 13

123

For Paul, the abundant life was Christ who was in Him. Paul teaches us that Christ is our abundance. Christ is all we need. He is the bread of life.

You want to understand what it means to be a servant of the Lord? Study Paul. You want to understand what it means to suffer for the Lord? Study Paul.

You want to study Paul? Read his letters. Paul is human in his letters. Paul shares his weaknesses, struggles and shortcomings. Paul's goal, however, is to put our focus on Jesus. As you study Paul's faith and his words, keep your eyes fixed on Jesus. Paul lets us see how God worked in his life so we can believe Him to work in our lives.

When I am struggling, Paul is a friend who encourages me in my faith in the Lord. I read his words to remind me of God's faithfulness to me in Christ. His words place my focus on what God is doing. The Christian life is not something I live, but it is Christ living in me. Paul's faith and life is a witness for my faith. Paul wrote:

> *"The things you have learned and received and*
> *heard and seen in me, practice these things;*
> *and the God of peace shall be with you."*
> *Philippians 4:9*

CHAPTER 24

JESUS

"Then Jesus was led up by the Spirit into the wilderness to be tempted by the devil. And after He had fasted forty days and forty nights, He then became hungry. And the tempter came and said to Him 'If You are the Son of God, command that these stones become bread.' But He answered and said, 'It is written, 'Man shall not live on bread alone, but on every word that proceeds out of the mouth of God." Then the devil took Him into the holy city; and he had Him stand on the pinnacle of the temple, and said to Him, 'If You are the Son of God throw Yourself down; for it is written, 'He will give His angels charge concerning You'; and 'On their hands they will bear You up, Lest You strike Your foot against a stone." Jesus said to him, 'On the other hand, it is written, 'You shall not put the Lord your God to the test." Again, the devil took Him to a very high mountain, and showed Him all the kingdoms of the world, and their glory; and he said to Him, 'All these things will I give You, if You fall down and worship me.' Then Jesus said to him, 'Begone, Satan! For it is written, 'You shall worship the Lord your*

> *God, and serve Him only." Then the devil left Him; and*
> *behold, angels came and began to minister to Him."*
> Matthew 4:1-11

Jesus had a wilderness journey. If He had a wilderness journey, how much more do we need one? We can learn a lot from His experience and how He used the word of God to face temptation.

Satan tempted Jesus three times. Jesus resisted the temptation each time using the word of God to communicate the will of God. Jesus stayed focused on God's will not His own. We will look at each temptation.

Temptation 1

Jesus had fasted for forty days and nights. He was hungry. It was only natural that Satan's first temptation would be food. It was where Jesus was the weakest at the moment. Satan likes to attack where we are weakest.

It is interesting that Satan says that if you are the Son of God, then do what God can do. You, son of God, turn these stones to bread and eat. Jesus responded:

> *"Man shall not live on bread alone, but on every*
> *word that proceeds out of the mouth of God."*
> Matthew 4:4

Jesus does not address whether or not He is the Son of God. He does not address whether or not He can turn the stone to bread. He addresses His submission to the will of God.

Jesus was more concerned with spiritual bread than physical bread. Being true to the will of God was more important to Him, than His hunger for physical food.

It is interesting when you consider that Adam and Eve put the fruit ahead of God's will. Esau put his hunger ahead of his birthright.

Jesus' birthright would have allowed Him to do what Satan asked. However, God's will was more important than His birthright.

Do we recognize our need for the spiritual food of God's word? Is God's will for our lives more important than our perceived physical needs? Christ is the bread of life (John 6:35).

Temptation 2

While in the first temptation, Satan did not use the word of God, he did in the second temptation. He used scripture that specifically related to the angels charge to care for Jesus. Satan knows the word of God. It actually scares me a bit to think that Satan knows the word of God better than I do.

Satan again challenged Jesus by saying, "If you are the Son of God." He knows Jesus is the Son of God. Satan was just trying to provoke Jesus to sin. If Satan can get Jesus to sin, his birth is pointless. His mission to save us from sin is thwarted.

Jesus again answered with the word of God:

> "You shall not put the Lord your God to the test."
> Matthew 4:7

As in the first temptation, Jesus did not address whether or not He is the Son of God or whether or not Satan accurately used the word of God. He just answered with the word of God. He again submitted Himself to the will of the Father.

Christ was demonstrating that He did not come to do His will, but the will of His Father who sent Him. Christ stayed in submission to God in spite of the fact He could have done what Satan was suggesting. He waited on the Father.

I am intrigued by the verse Jesus chose. We are not to test God. I wonder if we test God when we tell God we are doing something and His word promises that He will do this in response. I wonder if we are really acting in faith or just trying to manipulate God. Are we doing what God has called us to do? Or, are we trying to get God to do what we want Him to do?

Jesus knew that the angels would do what Satan proposed. Jesus also knew it was not the will of God for Him to throw Himself down. We need to be careful that we are applying His promises in submission to His will.

Temptation 3

Satan next promised to give everything within his domain to Jesus, if Jesus will just bow down and worship him. This time he did not say, 'If you are the Son of God.' This time he did not ask Jesus to do something to prove who He was. Instead, he promised to give Jesus power and authority, which is attractive to a sinner. Jesus, however, was not a sinner and responded:

> *"You shall worship the Lord your*
> *God, and serve Him only."*
> *Matthew 4:10*

Jesus again simply responded with the word of God. He did not question whether or not Satan could give him what he promised. Jesus simply stated the will of God with the word of God.

Reflection

As I reflect on how Jesus handled the temptations, I think of the passage in Ephesians concerning the armor of God:

> *"in addition to all, taking up the shield of faith with*
> *which you will be able to extinguish all the flaming*
> *missiles of the evil one. And take the helmet of salvation,*
> *and the sword of the Spirit, which is the word of God."*
> *Ephesians 6:16, 17*

I believe that because of Jesus' faith in His father that He really was never tempted. His shield of faith extinguished the fire of any temptation presented by Satan. He also used the sword of the Spirit which is the word of God.

What a wonderful example for us. Jesus did not feel the need to argue with Satan, or correct Satan, or teach Satan the error of His ways. Jesus simply stated the word of God as was appropriate for the temptation. Jesus relied on the power of the word of God.

I just said two key things. One, He used the word of God appropriately for the temptation. He needed to know the word of God to do that. We need to know the word of God to do that.

Two, He relied on the power of the word of God. We need to rely on the power of the word of God. We need to rely on it for our lives and for the lives of others.

The power to save is in God's word, not our ability to explain God's word. Jesus did not try to explain God's word, He simply stated it. The writer of Hebrews tells us:

> *"For the word of God is living and active and sharper*
> *than any two-edged sword, and piercing as far as the*
> *division of soul and spirit, of both joints and marrow, and*
> *able to judge the thoughts and intentions of the heart."*
> *Hebrews 4:12*

Jesus faced temptation with the word of God. We need to know the word of God and do the same. We need to have more than knowledge of the word of God. We need to have experience with God's faithfulness to His word. We need to experience God through His word.

We need to ask God to put His word in our hearts and our minds. Our minds that we might know it in time of need. Our hearts so that we will believe it. God works through His word. Christ is the word of God (John 1).

In closing, it is interesting that Jesus' wilderness journey ended with angels ministering to Him. Satan's second temptation was regarding the angels care of Jesus. Jesus waited on God and God was faithful.

WE ARE HIS GOOD WORK

"For I am confident of this very thing, that
He who began a good work in you will
perfect it until the day of Christ Jesus."
Philippians 1:6

CHAPTER 25

MY STORY

*"Upon Thee I was cast from birth; Thou hast
been my God from my mother's womb."*
Psalms 22:10

As long as I can remember, I have always believed in God. I was raised to believe in God. I was raised Catholic and my earliest recollection of knowing I believed something was when I went to confession for the first time. I was eight years old and had to confess sin to the priest.

I really couldn't think of a sin, so I lied to the priest so I could confess the lie. The priest instructed me to say ten Hail Mary prayers and ten Our Father prayers for the forgiveness of my sin.

I said the ten Our Father prayers because it was the Lord's Prayer found in the Bible. However, I only said Hail Mary ten times and did not say the prayer. The prayer is not in the Bible. The priest noticed and was not very happy with me. I was assigned ten more Hail Mary prayers.

I was bold enough to ask why I needed to do anything if Christ died on the cross for my sins. I got sent home and mom got a phone call from the priest. Yes, at a young age I was inquisitive about things of the Lord.

My next serious encounter of faith was when I was fifteen. I was sitting on a step in the backyard of my home and basically told God that if this was as good as life got, He could take me home. I was not enjoying life too much. God made a promise that He had a plan for my life. I accepted that answer. The verse I claim to this day is:

> *"'For I know the plans that I have for you,'*
> *declares the Lord, 'plans for welfare and not for*
> *calamity to give you a future and a hope.'"*
> *Jeremiah 29:11*

Jeremiah 29:11 has helped me trust God through many a trial. When I have doubted my life station, God has always reminded me that He has a plan.

At the age of eighteen, I had reached my goal in life (notice that I said my goal). I was working at NASA as an engineer. It was so exciting. That is also the first time I felt a cloud over my heart that told me God had another plan for my life.

As a senior in college, I knew that cloud meant that I was to submit my life to the Lordship of Christ (another serious encounter of faith). Up to this point, I only understood that Christ died for my sins and God had a plan for my life. Up to this time, I always trusted God had the rest figured out and did not think about it much.

As my Lord, He changed how I made decisions. Faith was now very important. And, by faith, I believed God wanted me to go into fulltime service for Him and thus, turned down the many engineering jobs I was offered. I served as a missionary for the next ten years of my life.

The final two years as a missionary I spent in Greece. That was a very good experience for me. All my strengths were useless to me because I could not communicate. I had to rely on the Lord. Good for all of us to learn. When our strengths are of no use to us we tend to rely on the Lord more. The verse that comes to mind is:

"I am the vine, you are the branches; he who
abides in Me, and I in him, he bears much fruit;
for apart from Me you can do nothing."
John 15:5

In Greece, I could do nothing. God worked in my life. As a side note, I got to go to Philippi and see what most likely was Paul's prison cell and the amphitheater in which he spoke. I also got to see the chariot ruts in the marble streets. While the city was just ruins, it did give me new appreciation for the time period.

While in Greece, another cloud comes over my heart and I left the mission field to get a Master's degree in Counseling. I worked at a large church while getting my degree. The degree helped me get a job at a private university which led to a job in the department that managed construction. As a woman managing construction, God taught me more than a few lessons.

It was while managing construction projects that I got my Master's degree in Engineering Management and my Professional Engineering License in Mechanical Engineering. God was using my education for His glory.

I often reflect on the fact that people were shocked that I would give up my engineering career to serve the Lord. My response was that God would make me an engineer again if that was part of His plan. Well, he did just that. God is amazing.

Another cloud comes over my heart and I move to Sacramento, California. I was hired as an engineer. Over time I managed three departments.

Throughout my story, God has been faithful. As a missionary, I had to reach out to people who would be willing to support my ministry. While I was terrible at raising support, my needs were always met.

As I studied for my various degrees, God always granted me success. Working full-time and studying is a difficult thing. I knew my job was to be faithful to study and the rest was up to God. God was faithful. When it came to the exams for my engineering license, God was oh so faithful.

I marvel at how God has blessed me. My career has not been the typical path for a woman. Women majored in engineering, yes. Mechanical Engineering, no. I managed construction as a construction manager.

God blessed me with success in everything He called me to do. And that is the point of faith….God put me in the work situations just as He had Joseph sold into slavery and thrown into prison. God was accomplishing something in me for His plan for me.

Do I understand it all? No. I do see that the experiences have made me confident to stand up for what I believe. I am not easily intimidated. Trust me when I say that men tried to intimidate me. I learned to stand firm. God was my rock.

If I had to choose two truths that have been most imprinted upon God's walk with me it is that He is faithful and He forgives. I am a sinner and get it wrong. God, however, is forgiving and always gets it right.

God has never failed me. There are so many times that I should have failed, but God gave me success. He is always faithful. His faithfulness is because of who He is and not because of who I am.

You will notice that I said a cloud was over my heart each time a major change was involved in God's walk with me. It really is the only way I can explain what I felt. As I wrote about the Israeli nation, I thought about the cloud over the tabernacle. That is how God has lead me.

I am in a place where I feel God is setting His plan for me in motion. Everything that has transpired in my life (good and bad) was preparing me for this time. It is fascinating to me that the bad is as much a part of God's plan for my life as is the good. The Apostle Paul said it oh so well:

"And we know that God causes all things to work
together for good to those who love God, to those
who are called according to His purpose."
Romans 8:28

Even the bad in my life God has worked toward my good. It is
an overwhelming thought. My sin He has worked toward my good.
The sin of others against me, He has worked toward my good.

Accepting the bad as part of God's plan is a struggle. How can
God allow the bad? I think the better question is why did God
protect me from worse? Why did He choose to save me?

I am working through the impact of past wounds on whom I
am today. The way I explain it to people is that at salvation God
removed the veil on my heart that separated me from Him. Now,
he is removing the veil on my heart that separates me from others.
Actually, the veil that protects me from others.

God wants us to be real. That does not mean that you see me
fully as God sees me, but I can trust God's protection of me and not
protect myself. Our vulnerability with others is not based on their
trustworthiness but on God's. I cannot say it is an easy lesson for me,
but I can say that I trust in the faithfulness of my God.

In the next several chapters, I will be sharing other truths God
has taught me on my journey. My hope is that they will help you
on your journey.

CHAPTER 26

CHRIST IS THE GOOD IN US

"For I know that nothing good dwells in me,
that is, in my flesh; for the wishing is present
in me, but the doing of the good is not."
Romans 7:18

Hopefully, all of us will agree that we are sinners. However, to say "nothing good dwells in me" is harder. It is the Apostle Paul who said it. The Apostle Paul is right. There is nothing good in us apart from Christ.

I knew I was a sinner but didn't give much thought to the concept that God would not see any good in me. I was a good person, at least by man's standard. The standard by which we measure ourselves is the key to our so-called goodness. By man's standards, I was a good person. By God's standard, nothing good dwells in me.

I am learning to see myself by God's standards. The good news as a Christian is that I have Christ in me and that is good. That is the only good that dwells in me. When God looks at me, He sees Christ and says it is good. Am I okay that Christ is the only good in me? I am better than okay, but it has been a process. I am more secure knowing that the good in me is Christ. I can never meet God's standard of performance; in Christ, I don't have to.

However, before I could see that the only good in me is Christ, I needed to see that nothing good dwelled in me. I had to come to the realization that even my strengths were weaknesses in God's walk with me. It is something I need to be reminded of every day.

I think the Apostle Peter is a good witness of this lesson. He was always ready to go to battle for the Lord. Even in the garden of Gethsemane as the Lord was being betrayed he had his sword ready. Then, in the court when Christ was on trial, Peter denied the Lord three times.

Peter, after failing the Lord, saw his need for the power of the Lord in his life. Peter's power could accomplish nothing. God's power can accomplish everything. We need the power of the Lord. We do not understand that until our power fails.

In Acts, there is a different Peter. His confidence is no longer in himself but in the Lord. He now possessed the power of the Lord. In that power, he was a great witness for the Lord. The Lord wants to do the same in our lives. He wants our confidence to be in Christ not in ourselves.

Remember what we learned as we studied Paul:

> *"although I myself might have confidence even in the flesh. If anyone else has a mind to put confidence in the flesh, I far more...More than that, I count all things to be loss in view of the surpassing value of knowing Christ Jesus my Lord, for whom I have suffered the loss of all things, and count them but rubbish in order that I may gain Christ, and may be found in Him, not having a righteousness of my own derived from the Law, but that which is through faith in Christ, the righteousness which comes from God on the basis of faith,"*
> *Philippians 3:4-9*

Paul considered everything in his flesh that he could boast about as rubbish compared to knowing Christ in him. When we rely on good in us, we are not relying on Christ. We don't need Christ if we are good. Peter learned that. We need to learn that.

The Psalmist said:

> *"Hear my prayer, O Lord, Give ear to my supplications!*
> *Answer me in Thy faithfulness, in Thy righteousness!*
> *And do not enter into judgment with Thy servant,*
> *For in Thy sight no man living is righteous."*
> *Psalms 143:1, 2*

In God's sight, no man living is righteous. No man is good in himself/herself. We need the righteousness that is found through faith in Christ Jesus.

It is humbling to realize that there is no good in us. Our best falls so short of the standard of God. God wants us to be so much more. As you ponder the good in you, please keep in mind God's standard of measure. God is the standard.

The amazing thing about God's plan is that we have the goodness of Christ in us. We have the greatest goodness one can possess. God's plan is not to humiliate us, but to exalt us in Christ. He doesn't want us to feel our nothingness, but everything we have in Christ.

To live in Christ, however, we must die to self. That is what Christ meant when He said:

> *"If anyone wishes to come after Me, let him deny himself,*
> *and take up his cross, and follow Me. For whoever*
> *wishes to save his life shall lose it; but whoever loses*
> *his life for My sake and the gospel's shall save it."*
> *Mark 8:34, 35*

Now did Christ expect us to actually carry a cross? No. Did Christ actually expect us to lose our lives? No. We are still alive and so were His disciples. Christ was not discussing something physical. He was discussing something spiritual.

Christ was telling us that our reason for life needed to be Him and not ourselves. He was telling us that we needed to submit our wills to His will. He was telling us that we needed to rest in His strength and not our own. I was following Jesus until that last one about His strength not mine.

As long as I was doing it for the Lord wasn't I okay? Isn't being a Christian about living for the Lord? Christ would say yes if it is Him living it through us. If we are living it in our strength, it is not the Christian life. Jesus said:

> *"I am the vine, you are the branches; he who*
> *abides in Me, and I in him, He bears much fruit;*
> *for apart from Me you can do nothing."*
> *John 15:5*

And the Apostle Paul wrote:

> *"He made Him who knew no sin to be sin on our behalf,*
> *that we might become the righteousness of God in Him."*
> *2 Corinthians 5:21*

The Christian life is about Christ living it in and through us. All good in me is Christ. All good I do is Christ through me. Everything I do apart from the power of Christ is rubbish in the eyes of God. I need to measure the flesh by God's standards and let go of any good I think exists within me. I need to let go and recognize that God wants complete sovereignty in my life. Only His complete sovereignty in my life meets His standard. Self needs to die so Christ can live.

I am still learning this lesson. I am also learning that to know Christ and know Him completely is the abundant life.

CHAPTER 27

EMOTIONS ARE EMOTIONS

"Be angry, and yet do not sin; do not let the sun go down
on your anger, and do not give the devil an opportunity."
Ephesians 4:26, 27

Emotions are emotions. Emotions become a problem for us when we let the emotions take root in our hearts and influence our choices. We need to feel but we don't need to let emotions control us.

When bitterness takes root in our hearts, we become bitter people. When jealousy takes root in our hearts, we typically sin against the person of whom we are jealous. Ephesians 4:26, 27 provides good advice on how to handle emotions.

First, it teaches us to feel the emotion but not to sin. The verses say, 'be angry.' The emotion, however, should not dictate our choices, 'and yet do not sin.' Happiness can be just as dangerous as anger. When we are happy we don't always feel the same need for God.

Denying emotions is not the answer. We need to feel the emotions, so we can move on. Again, the emotion is not bad in and of itself. The problem is when we give power to the emotion so that sin becomes a consequence.

We need to get the emotion out so it loses power over us. Did you know that a lie we believe in our heads loses power when we speak it out loud? The truth gains power when we speak it out loud. We need to get the emotions out before they become our truth rather than the word of God. We get the emotion out by confessing it to God. Sometimes it helps to also confess it to someone we trust.

Second, we need to put our emotions in the right perspective before going to sleep (my interpretation of not letting the sun go down). For me, this means putting the emotion at the foot of Christ's throne. It means putting the emotion in submission to the will of Christ. The emotion may not go away but it has been entrusted to the Lord; it is in submission to the Lord.

I believe we are more vulnerable to our emotions and the attacks of Satan when we sleep. I believe emotions are more easily manipulated when we sleep. Think about it, we let our guards down to fall asleep. We need to be right with God before we go to asleep.

I learned this concept when I stopped practicing transcendental meditation. I quickly learned that my mantra was not just a word but the name of a spirit. A spirit that did not serve God.

My mantra did not give up easily. I stopped meditating, but my mantra kept trying to get my attention. If it was just a word (I had been told it was just a word when I started), you would think it would have been easy. My sleep was haunted. I would wake up screaming my mantra to make it lose power.

I started memorizing verses before I went to sleep to use in response to the scenes that played out in my sleep. I started clutching my Bible while I slept. What the Apostle Paul described in Ephesians played out in my sleep:

> "For our struggle is not against flesh and blood, but
> against the rulers, against the powers, against the

> *world forces of this darkness, against the spiritual*
> *forces of wickedness in the heavenly places."*
> Ephesians 6:12

Fortunately, quoting scripture and clinging to the word of God while I slept worked. God, through Christ, gave me victory as He promised. I did learn a valuable lesson: Get things right with God before I fall asleep. Our emotions do carry over into our dreams.

Thirdly, the verse tells us not to give Satan an opportunity. Did you ever consider that your emotions give Satan an opportunity? When our emotions are strong, we want to act on them. We need to pause and let God dictate our actions and not our emotions. When we allow our emotions to make our choices, we give Satan an opportunity.

Emotions are just emotions. God gave us the ability to feel and we need to feel our emotions. It is not a sin to feel. While we are feeling, we need to submit our choices to the will of God. We need God to walk with us through the emotions, so that we do not sin and do not give Satan an opportunity.

I feel strongly. I place my emotions before God and ask that He keep me strong in Him while I feel. I need to feel. I do not need to sin. I am not saying it is easy. God, in Christ, does give me the victory.

I have to admit that my emotions don't always just go away. There have been times when it has been a long process for God to walk me through my feelings. He is ever faithful.

I would like to paraphrase the Ephesian verses to say, 'Feel but do not sin. Give your feelings to the Lord throughout the day and again before you sleep. Claim God's promise to protect you, so that Satan cannot tempt you into evil.' Please don't quote my paraphrase. I provide it only as a way of considering the verses as it relates to your emotions.

I feel I must add that God wants us to feel. He wants us to feel His joy, hope in Him, peace that surpasses understanding and so much more. As we fix our eyes on Jesus, we will feel the greatest emotions we can feel. I close with:

> *"Peace I leave with you; My peace I give to you;*
> *not as the world gives you, do I give to you. Let not*
> *your heart be troubled, nor let it be fearful."*
> *John 14:27*

CHAPTER 28

INTIMATE FRIENDS

*"Two are better than one because they have a good
return for their labor. For if either of them falls,
the one will lift up his companion. But woe to the
one who falls when there is not another to lift him
up. Furthermore, if two lie down together they keep
warm, but how can one be warm alone? And if one
can overpower him who is alone, two can resist him.
A cord of three strands is not quickly torn apart."*
Ecclesiastes 4:9-12

These verses are commonly used in the context of a marriage, which is appropriate. It is also appropriate to apply them in the context of friendship. We need friends. We need trustworthy intimate friends who build us up and support us.

When I was graduating from high school, a former good friend came to me as graduation was approaching and asked if we could talk. She explained how the friends a person chooses makes all the difference in the world. She said that she chose the wrong friends. She asked me to remember that.

I have remembered. Through the course of God working in my life, I have learned that the friends we choose does make a difference. The Apostle Paul warned us:

> *"Do not be deceived: 'Bad company*
> *corrupts good morals.'"*
> 1 Corinthians 15:33

I have not found a verse that says good company corrects bad morals. The people who become our dearest and closest friends have an impact on who we become. The people we feel the safest with whom to bear our souls have influence over our decisions. We need to pick those friends carefully.

I call those dear close friends, intimate friends. There is a difference between a friend and an intimate friend. An intimate friend is someone with whom I can share my secrets and they are safe. An intimate friend is someone who encourages me in my faith. An intimate friend is someone who is with me at my lowest point and helps me stay centered in God's will for me.

God knows we need intimate friends. Ecclesiastes 4:9-12 make it clear that we are better off when we have intimate friends with whom we can share our burdens. The writer of Hebrews said:

> *"Let us hold fast the confession of our hope without*
> *wavering, for He who promised is faithful; and let*
> *us consider how to stimulate one another to love and*
> *good deeds, not forsaking our own assembling together,*
> *as is the habit of some, but encouraging one another;*
> *and all the more, as you see the day drawing near."*
> Hebrews 10:23-25

As Christians, we need the encouragement of other Christians to stimulate us to 'love and good deeds.' We need one another. It's important who we choose to be those intimate friends. It's important that we are that type of friend.

Intimate friends are able to confront one another in regards to sin. It isn't easy and yet, it is an act of love. Intimate friends also struggle with one another as they get victory over the sin.

Intimate friends are willing to stand by one another in faith and pray with each other. Intimate friends do not let each other be alone in the battle of living the Christian life. We trust God with each other and for each other.

Ecclesiastes tells us that we need to lift each other up when we fall. We need to help each other stand firm when under attack. We need to help each other resist temptation. We need to provide God's love and support to see friends to victory in faith.

We all need to have a good company of intimate friends. Friends who have our spiritual standards. Friends who have our moral standards. Proverbs states it well:

"Iron sharpens iron, So one man sharpens another."
Proverbs 27:17

We need to select intimate friends who sharpen us in the Lord. I have to be honest, I am very selective of whom I call my closest and dearest friends. I have relaxed in terms of who I will call a friend. I have not relaxed in terms of whom I call an intimate friend. I don't easily trust others with my innermost thoughts and feelings.

Those I call my intimate friends, I need. I depend on them to keep me honest with myself. I depend on them to give me sound advice. I depend on them to support me when I am down. I am fortunate, because my intimate friends do that and so much more. They also understand that God's walk with me must come first in my life. I also try to be that kind of friend for them.

What I have said is not to discourage any of us from being friends with people whom God places in our paths. We should always be ready to extend God's love and forgiveness. This truth is about intimate friends. Friends we entrust with our true selves. Friends that can encourage us in God's walk with us.

CHAPTER 29

WE WILL STRUGGLE

"So then, my beloved, just as you have always obeyed,
not as in my presence only, but now much more
in my absence, work out your salvation with fear
and trembling; for it is God who is at work in you,
both to will and to work for His good pleasure."
Philippians 2:12, 13

Philippians 2:12, 13 tells us to work out our salvation. The word work implies that it will take effort and perseverance on our part. It also implies that it won't be easy.

The Christian life is not easy. It's easier for some than others, but it is not easy for anyone if they pursue Christ being Lord of their lives. The Apostle Paul explains the struggle well in Romans 7. The flesh has its desires which are not concerned with the will of God and the Holy Spirit has its desires which are according to the will of God. This conflict between the flesh and the Spirit of God makes for interesting struggles in the life of a believer.

In an earlier chapter, I mentioned my involvement in transcendental meditation and the battle that ensued as I quit. I had my mantra trying to remove any thoughts of God and fortunately,

God not budging. I remember one specific dream where I asked if either side wanted my opinion. My opinion was that I would rather think about God. My mantra did not care what I wanted.

It was a battle. It was a scary battle. I was working out my salvation with fear and trembling.

Fortunately for me, God was at work in me. He was winning the battle on my behalf. I, however, had to endure the battle. I can boast in the victory the Lord gave me. As the Apostle John stated:

> *"You are from God, little children, and have*
> *overcome them; because greater is He who*
> *is in you than he who is in the world."*
> *1 John 4:4*

God is greater.

Most of my struggles are not so dramatic with visible spiritual warfare. Most of them involve me wanting one thing and God's word reminding me to trust God and His faithfulness.

For example, that person who sabotages me at work. My first thought is to get even. The first thought is that that person will regret the day he/she messed with me. However, the Apostle Paul tells us:

> *"Never pay back evil for evil to anyone. Respect*
> *what is right in the sight of all men. If possible,*
> *so far as it depends on you, be at peace with all*
> *men. Never take your own revenge, beloved, but*
> *leave room for the wrath of God, for it is written,*
> *'Vengeance is Mine, I will repay,' says the Lord."*
> *Romans 12:17-19*

My struggle has begun. I want revenge and God says vengeance is His. Not only that, I am to be at peace with this individual. Oh, I am struggling. My salvation is being worked out in me.

Or, how about that co-worker whose messes you are always being asked to clean up, only to learn that he/she will be promoted to be your boss. The promotion is not because they are more qualified. And, the administration is expecting you to make sure the person succeeds. What?

Philippians 1:12-13 says it is God at work in us for His good pleasure. It definitely does not say for my pleasure. My job has nothing to do with what I or my boss wants, but everything to do with what God wants. Will I submit to what God wants?

Joseph was a slave and then a prisoner. Joseph served for other people's success. Ouch, I guess I know what I am supposed to do. Joseph is a witness to me of what it means to serve God in the workplace.

I think of Jonathan's willingness to support David. Jonathan was the rightful heir to the throne in man's world. Jonathan understood, however, that God had a different plan. He stepped aside and supported God's choice. We need to realize that God has His plan in our workplace.

Jesus told Pilate:

> *"You would have no authority over Me, unless it*
> *had been given you from above; for this reason he*
> *who delivered Me up to you has the greater sin."*
> *John 19:11*

Pilate had tried to explain to Jesus the power he had over Jesus' situation. Jesus explains to Pilate that he only has authority because God gave it to him. Jesus acknowledged that it was God who was in control of the situation regardless of how it looked to Pilate and others. We need to understand that God is in control.

The nice thing is that in the midst of my struggles God walks with me. He walks with you in the midst of your struggles. He does not abandon us in our struggles. The struggles help us relinquish control to the Holy Spirit in us. The struggles do not define us. God's walk with us defines us. God is working in us that we might be His light in this dark world. Changes come with a struggle.

I believe Jesus struggled in the Garden of Gethsemane when he prayed:

> *"My Father, if it is possible, let this cup pass from*
> *Me; yet not as I will, but as Thou wilt."*
> *Matthew 26:39*

We are told in Mark 14:34 that His soul was 'deeply grieved to the point of death.' The Gospel of Luke tells us:

> *"And being in agony He was praying very*
> *fervently; and His sweat became like drops of*
> *blood, falling down upon the ground."*
> *Luke 22:44*

Jesus did the will of God in spite of the agony, in spite of being grieved with what He was about to face. He understands that we will struggle with doing the will of God. He told His disciples:

> *"Keep watching and praying, that you may not enter into*
> *temptation; the spirit is willing, but the flesh is weak."*
> *Matthew 26:41*

The flesh is weak. The flesh will struggle against the will of God. The spirit is willing. The two battle for control. Christ tells us to keep watch and pray. We will be faced with temptation. When we are in those struggles we need to pray. The Apostle Paul exhorts us:

> *"But I say, walk by the Spirit, and you will not*
> *carry out the desire of the flesh. For the flesh sets its*
> *desire against the Spirit, and the Spirit against the*

> *flesh; for these are in opposition to one another, so*
> *that you may not do the things that you please."*
> Galatians 5:16-17

Struggling is part of the Christian walk. Fortunately, we have Christ, through the Holy Spirit, in us to give us victory. The flesh wants control and Christ wants control. Through prayer by faith we give Christ control.

Do not be surprised that you struggle. I use to think that because I struggled something was wrong with me. Now, I know something is very right with me. My flesh is losing in its struggle against the will of God. I am growing in my faith. God is working out His will for me for His good pleasure.

It is an amazing thought that God is having pleasure in me. The God of the universe is finding pleasure in who I am in Christ.

Give your struggles to God. He will give you victory. You will experience His pleasure in who you are becoming in Christ.

CHAPTER 30

PRAYING THE WILL OF GOD

"And this is the confidence which we have before
Him, that, if we ask anything according to His
will, He hears us. And if we know that He hears
us in whatever we ask, we know that we have the
requests which we have asked from Him."
1 John 5:14, 15

Prayer plays an integral role in God's relationship with us. It is how we communicate with God our Father. It is more than prayer requests. It is about spending time with God. Unlike others in our lives, God is always available to listen to us and communicate with us. It is an amazing blessing that God is always available to us.

I have probably read more books on the subject of prayer than any other topic. As I have read and listened to people discuss prayer, I have often felt like the measure of a good prayer life was determined by whether or not God answered the prayers as prayed.

It was a struggle for me to get to a place in my relationship with God where I learned that the measure of a good prayer life is submission to God's will and faith in God. I don't trust my prayer. I don't trust my faith. I trust God.

God answers all prayers according to His will. God answers because God promised He would answer. The goal is not the answer. The goal of prayer is submission to the will of God. The promise is that we will come to know God and His will.

Prayer should not be about getting God to do what we want. It is about us bringing all our joys and concerns to Him knowing that He cares. It is seeking God's will in everything.

I do not have children but I have friends that do. One of the saddest days for parents is when their children no longer come to them with everything. Parents want to be the first people with whom their child shares their victories and sorrows.

God, our Heavenly Father, is that same kind of parent. He wants us, as His children, to turn to Him first. Sadly, we usually do not turn to Him until we have exhausted every other possibility. In the wilderness, we learn to turn to Him first.

When I pray for myself and others, I do not always know what God's will is for the situation. I don't know how He wants to reveal His glory in the situation, so I ask that His will be done. Sometimes, I just pray through His word.

In His word, God has given us promises that we know are His will for His children. These promises we can pray with confidence "that we have the requests which we have asked from Him," because they are according to His will. We need to pray these promises for ourselves and others. We can also pray the Lord's Prayer for the church of God.

As we look at a few promises, consider people in your life for whom you can pray. Consider other promises you can pray.

Promise of Peace

> *"Be anxious for nothing, but in everything by prayer*
> *and supplication with thanksgiving let your requests*

be made known to God. And the peace of God,
which surpasses all comprehension, shall guard
your hearts and your minds in Christ Jesus."
Philippians 4:6, 7

I purposefully picked this promise first. Peace awaits us as when we give our concerns to God. Often all we need is the peace of knowing that God is in control; the peace that God will accomplish that which concerns us. God is in control of everything we have brought to Him. When we feel anxious, we can pray for His peace. He wants us to have peace.

He wants His peace to control us, not our anxiety. When we give into our anxieties, they become gods to us. We can only have one God. God needs to be our God and not our anxieties. We need to give people's anxieties to God and ask that He give them peace.

Promise of Bearing the Fruit of the Spirit

"But the fruit of the Spirit is love, joy, peace, patience,
kindness, goodness, faithfulness, gentleness, self-
control; against such things there is no law."
Galatians 5:22, 23

As I was thinking about this verse, I was reminded of what the Apostle John said:

"You did not choose Me, but I chose you, and appointed
you, that you should go and bear fruit, and that
your fruit should remain, that whatever you ask of
the Father in My name, He may give to you."
John 15:16

It is God's will that we bear the fruit of the Spirit and that it remain. It's not a seasonal fruit we bear. It is a fruit for all seasons.

It's a fruit we bear because of Christ. We do not produce the fruit but the Spirit of Christ in us produces the fruit.

We need to pray these Galatians verses for ourselves and others. Here is a way we can pray it:

Thank you, Father, that in Christ, through the Holy Spirit, my life bears the fruit of love, joy, peace, patience, kindness, goodness, faithfulness, gentleness, and self-control. Thank You that in Christ the fruit remains and endures day after day.

Instead of the word "my," you can place the name of someone you are praying for. What an awesome prayer we can pray for one another. We have the confidence God will answer it, because it is according to His will for His children.

As you pray this prayer and other prayers for people, please remember that God's walk with us is over a lifetime. Changes take time. The important thing to remember in faith, is that God does accomplish the work.

Promise of Faith

> *"fixing our eyes on Jesus, the author*
> *and perfecter of faith."*
> *Hebrews 12:2*

It was hard picking one verse for faith. I chose this one because I like how it says 'fixing our eyes on Jesus.' We walk in the direction our eyes lead us. We need to walk in the direction of Christ.

We so often tie answers to prayer to the amount of faith one has. That bothers me. None of us can have perfect faith. What is enough faith?

I think of the story found in Mark 9 when Jesus asks the father of a demon possessed son if he believed. The father said:

"I do believe; help my unbelief."
Mark 9:24

Jesus answered his prayer. Jesus will answer our prayers even though perfect faith is not possible for us. We need to keep our eyes on Jesus and trust Him to perfect our faith. He will build our faith because it is according to His will. We need to pray for faith for one another. We need to ask our Heavenly Father to fix our eyes on Jesus.

I have only looked at three verses. There are so many truths we can pray for ourselves and one another and know God will accomplish that which we have requested, because it is according to His will. Each day He will perfect in us these qualities until we are with Him in heaven.

Can you imagine if all these truths were being manifested in everyone who says he/she believes in Jesus? We would turn our world upside down. We need to focus our prayers on those truths we know are the will of God.

I do pray for people and their requests. I pray for God's will for them and His grace to sustain them. People need to know people are praying for them. I will tell God what I would like Him to do, but I always ask Him to accomplish His will.

I also pray His promises for me and others. I am mindful in my prayers that it is in Christ and through His Spirit that we change.

It is in Christ that Mary is love. Isn't it interesting that it doesn't say I love, but that I am love in Christ? There is a difference. Christ is the power behind the love and I bear the fruit of love. What a beautiful picture.

Think of people in your life for whom you can pray these and other promises. As you read the word of God look for His promises and pray them for you and others. Pray and watch God work.

As a reminder, the power that answers prayer is not with our prayer or with our faith. The power is with God. As we see answered prayer we are tempted to trust our prayer or our faith. We need to ever be mindful that it is God's faithfulness to His promises that is causing the work to be accomplished in us. He uses us in the process, but it is all Him.

CHAPTER 31

SATAN

"Be of sober spirit, be on the alert. Your
adversary, the devil, prowls about like a
roaring lion, seeking someone to devour."
1 Peter 5:8

A missionary who served in Africa shared a story in church one Sunday. From a distance he saw ten Africans standing completely still. It was not a normal scene so he looked closer and saw the lion. The lion was facing the Africans looking up and down the line the Africans formed. Eventually, the lion left.

The missionary spoke with one of his African friends about the scene that unfolded before his eyes. The friend explained that the lion understood that he was outnumbered. So, he was looking for the one person that showed fear and that was the one he would attack. Not seeing any fear, he retreated.

James said:

"Submit therefore to God. Resist the
devil and he will flee from you."
James 4:7

Satan does not have power over us. He will flee us if we stand firm in God. The Apostle John tells us:

"You are from God, little children, and have
overcome them; because greater is He who
is in you than he who is in the world."
1 John 4:4

Just before this verse in 1 John, the Apostle John is talking about testing the spirits. He is telling us that in Christ, we have overcome the evil spirits. He is telling us that Christ who is in us is greater than the devil. We can stand firm.

I fear that we give Satan too much credit or should I say blame (we are responsible for our sin). Satan is not all powerful. James tells us that if we resist he will flee. Flee is an active word.

Satan cannot be everywhere. He can only be in one place at a time. So, if he is bothering me, he cannot be bothering you. Yes, he does have help. His help, too, can only be in one place at a time.

I want us to read five very distinct passages in the Bible when Satan was involved in the lives of men.

Passage 1 - Adam and Eve:

"Now the serpent was more crafty than any beast of the
field which the Lord God had made. And he said to the
woman, "Indeed, has God said, "You shall not eat from
any tree of the garden"?" And the woman said to the
serpent, "From the fruit of the trees of the garden we may
eat; but from the fruit of the tree which is in the middle
of the garden, God has said, "You shall not eat from it
or touch it, lest you die."" And the serpent said to the
woman, "You surely shall not die! For God knows that
in the day you eat from it your eyes will be opened, and
you will be like God, knowing good and evil." When the

> *woman saw that the tree was good for food, and that it*
> *was a delight to the eyes, and that the tree was desirable*
> *to make one wise, she took from its fruit and ate; and*
> *she gave also to her husband with her, and he ate."*
> Genesis 3:1-6

It is interesting how Satan engaged Eve. He first stated God's will incorrectly by saying they could not eat the fruit of any tree. Eve wishing to correct him says that they can only not eat of tree in the middle of the garden. She does not identify the significance of the fruit but Satan knew.

Satan then goes on to say that it won't happen as God has said and that she can become like God by eating it. She now looks at the fruit of the tree differently and succumbs to temptation.

Satan knows the word of God. Satan will use the word of God incorrectly to tempt us into sin. We need to know it correctly to resist temptation.

Please note that Satan did not pick the fruit and hand it to Eve. He only tempted her. Eve did the rest.

Passage 2 - Job:

> *"Now there was a day when the sons of God came to*
> *present themselves before the Lord, and Satan also came*
> *among them. And the Lord said to Satan, 'From where*
> *do you come?' Then Satan answered the Lord and*
> *said, 'From roaming about on the earth and walking*
> *around on it.' And the Lord said to Satan, 'Have you*
> *considered My servant Job? For there is no one like him*
> *on the earth, a blameless and upright man, fearing God*
> *and turning away from evil.' Then Satan answered*
> *the Lord, 'Does Job fear God for nothing? Hast Thou*
> *not made a hedge about him and his house and all*
> *that he has, on every side? Thou hast blessed the work*

> *of his hands, and his possessions have increased in the*
> *land. But put forth Thy hand now and touch all that*
> *he has; he will surely curse Thee to Thy face.' Then*
> *the Lord said to Satan, 'Behold, all that he has is in*
> *your power, only do not put forth your hand on him.'*
> *So Satan departed from the presence of the Lord."*
> *Job 1:6-12*

Besides the fact that I find it so interesting that Satan was actually in the presence of God having a conversation with Him, I see three key truths in this passage. One, Satan knew who Job was and about his life. Two, he needed God's permission to do anything to Job. Three, God gave him permission. I believe that permission was based on the fact that God trusted Job's faith.

Passage 3 - Jesus:

> *"Then Jesus was led up by the Spirit into the wilderness*
> *to be tempted by the devil... Then the devil left Him; and*
> *behold angels came and began to minister to Him."*
> *Matthew 4:1, 11*

We have discussed Jesus' experience as Satan tempted Him. I want to add that after Jesus responded with the word of God to the three temptations, just as James 4:7 said, Satan fled.

Passage 4 - Peter:

> *"Simon, Simon, behold, Satan has demanded*
> *permission to sift you like wheat; but I have prayed for*
> *you, that your faith may not fail; and you, when once*
> *you have turned again, strengthen your brothers."*
> *Luke 22:31, 32*

Satan is not just asking for permission; Jesus says he is demanding permission. There were other disciples, but Satan wanted to sift Peter. Again, he needed permission to do anything.

Passage 5 - Paul:

> *"And because of the surpassing greatness of the*
> *revelations, for this reason, to keep me from exalting*
> *myself, there was given me a thorn in the flesh, a*
> *messenger of Satan to buffet me-to keep me from*
> *exalting myself! Concerning this I entreated the*
> *Lord three times that it might depart from me.*
> *And He has said to me, 'My grace is sufficient*
> *for you, for power is perfected in weakness.'"*
> 2 Corinthians 12:7-9

God permitted this messenger of Satan to remain a thorn in Paul's flesh. I like how Paul says it was given him. When God provided his answer to Paul's request, Paul gave thanks. God's answer was that His grace was sufficient for Paul.

Satan has no power over us. Anything Satan might think to do to us, he has to get God's permission. Most of the stuff we blame on Satan is either a result of our sin or the result of living in a sinful world. People get sick. People die. People are harmed by the sins of others.

We do have to be on the alert as Scripture tells us. We need to know the word of God to accurately defend against temptation and have the shield of faith to protect us from Satan's flaming missiles. But in the end, we need to rest in God and look to Him for our deliverance. He has won the war. His grace is sufficient.

I have shared the spiritual warfare I experienced as a result of transcendental meditation. I also experienced the power of God and the power of His word to give me victory. God is with us and will give us the strength to resist as we trust in Him.

CHAPTER 32

GRACE

"For the Lord God is a sun and shield; The Lord gives grace and glory; No good thing does He withhold from those who walk uprightly. O Lord of hosts, How blessed is the man who trusts in Thee!"
Psalms 84:11-12

We talk a lot about the role of grace at the time of salvation. However, it is also a life of grace that we must live in Christ. We don't just experience grace at salvation. We experience grace every day in God's walk with us, whether or not we realize it.

Grace is more than unconditional acceptance. It is more than forgiveness. It is a commitment of God to us in spite of us.

We are imperfect humans who get it wrong more often than not. God through His grace never fails to take us by the hand and walk with us. God through His grace is ever faithful to us.

We can do nothing perfectly. We can do nothing in the Christian life on our own. We can do nothing to the standard of God. Yet, God loves us and delivers us and provides for us and…Listen to what the Apostle Paul says:

"For I am the least of the apostles, who am not fit to be
called an apostle, because I persecuted the church of God.
But by the grace of God I am what I am, and His grace
toward me did not prove vain; but I labored even more
than all of them, yet not I, but the grace of God with me."
1 Corinthians 15:9, 10

Paul recognized that it was only by the grace of God that he was an apostle. He recognized that it was only by the grace of God that he labored.

I don't always recognize the grace of God. I don't recognize it because I don't think about it. Paul thought about it. Paul acknowledged his need for grace. I need God's grace. You need God's grace.

Paul beseeched the Lord three times to remove a throne in his flesh. Paul shares God's response:

"My grace is sufficient for you, for
power is perfected in weakness."
2 Corinthians 12:9

God considers His grace sufficient. His power is perfected when we are in need of His grace. We are in need of His grace every second of every day. God is teaching me that I find His power for living when I rest in His grace. Let me say that again, I find His power for living when I rest in His grace. The same is true for you.

Paul includes grace in his greetings in each of his letters to believers. Paul understood the need for believers to experience God's grace for living the Christian life.

The Apostle Peter wrote:

"You therefore, beloved, knowing this beforehand,
be on your guard lest, being carried away by the
error of unprincipled men, you fall from your own

> *steadfastness, but grow in the grace and knowledge*
> *of our Lord and Savior Jesus Christ. To Him be*
> *the glory, both now and to the day of eternity."*
> 2 Peter 3:17, 18

Peter encourages us to grow in grace. I read a book (I do not remember the name of the book) and it described grace as the rich soil in which God plants us so we can grow. Grace, like rich soil, provides everything needed for us to grow in Christ.

Grace is hard for us to grasp. We can define it, but to truly cling to it is difficult. Clinging to grace requires a recognition that nothing we do meets God's standards. Our best falls short. God accepts us in Christ by grace through faith. This is true at salvation and every day thereafter.

I know this truth in my head, but my heart hopes for something good in me. God's pleasure is a result of His grace in me through Jesus Christ. It is not me. This goes back to the truth that there is no good in me; it is hard to believe that about one's self. And yet, our joy is made complete when we rest in the truth that we are fully acceptable through Christ who died for us.

There is nothing I can do to please God. God's standard is holy perfection and I cannot produce holy perfection. Fortunately, in God's grace I do not have to. God asks for my heart and He produces the rest. Actually, it is a comforting place to be. My flesh, however, sometimes wants to feel there is something special about me.

There is nothing special about me except Christ in me. It is His grace that gives me continual access to God. I need to take my eyes off of me and fix them on Christ. His grace is sufficient.

The Apostle Paul assures us:

> *"There is therefore now no condemnation*
> *for those who are in Christ Jesus."*
> *Romans 8:1*

CHAPTER 33

MEDITATE ON THE WORD OF GOD

"This book of the law shall not depart from your
mouth, but you shall meditate on it day and night,
so that you may be careful to do according to all
that is written in it; for then you will make your
way prosperous, and then you will have success."
Joshua 1:8

I was reading the news this morning and they had a special on this foundation that is teaching kids in schools how to do transcendental meditation. I realized then that I needed to do a chapter on meditating on the word of God.

God protected me and shielded me from the dangers of this practice. To help me during those times when I was accustomed to meditating, I started meditating on God's word. I would take a verse and meditate on it. I would exclude all other thoughts except thoughts of God and His word.

The meditation involved saying a verse over and over in my mind. Sometimes other verses would come to me and I would repeat them over and over. The goal was to fill my mind with the word of God. I was not praying. I was focused on who God was by focusing on His word. Meditation is basically focused thinking.

This morning after I read the article, I went to my bedroom and meditated on God's word. I am reading in Romans and took a verse from the chapter I read:

"Thanks be to God through Jesus Christ our Lord!"
Romans 7:25

As I meditated on this verse over and over, I started thanking the Lord for everything I have in Christ. I thanked Him for the fruit of the Spirit. I thanked Him for His grace. I thanked Him for his salvation. I thanked him for rescuing me from the practice of transcendental meditation. Then more verses came to me. It was wonderful.

As Joshua 1:8 states, we need to mediate on God's word. We need to teach our children to meditate on the word of God. Meditation trains us to listen to God speak through His word.

There are several ways to approach meditating on God's word. You can do like I did this morning and pick a verse from the passage you are reading and keep repeating it to yourself.

You can pick a book of the Bible and read it and then meditate on what you read. It's been said that if you do this four times a day for a month you will memorize the book. I can testify that it does help in the memorization of a book.

You could pick a topic and meditate on different verses each time you meditate. Or, mediate on the same verse for several days or weeks.

Twenty minutes twice a day is the suggested time frame. However, do not worry about the amount of time. The goal is to be quiet before the Lord and ask Him to place His word in your heart. If you can, it is helpful to do it before you start the day and at the end of the day.

Basically, you repeat the verse over and over. As other verses come to mind, you can repeat them. Like I did this morning, you can start thanking the Lord for everything He is doing in your life and the lives of those around you. Focus on Him and His word.

This is not a time to pray for everyone, but a time for God to work His word into your life. As the Psalmist says:

> *"Cease striving and know that I am God."*
> Psalms 46:10

As we meditate, we find we settle into a peaceful state and 'cease striving.' We find God. We learn to listen to God's voice.

As we repeat God's word over and over it becomes a stronger part of our memory. When we need it in times of trouble it is there for us. The other wonderful news is that it gains power by being spoken out loud. When you can, say the verses our loud as you meditate. I find a soft whisper the best voice.

It is sad that I tried transcendental meditation. It was dangerous. God rescued me.

I did, however, learn the value of meditating on the word of God and the power of spiritual warfare. Meditating on God's word won the battle. Meditating on God's word provided the strength for the battle. His word in the power of the Holy Spirit is stronger than anything or anyone we will ever encounter.

Consider meditating on the word of God. Consider sitting quietly and reciting His word over and over to yourself. Consider putting everything out of your mind but the word of God for a moment of time in your day. It will change you. It has changed me.

An added bonus is that when I wake up I find myself reciting the word of God upon which I have been meditating. I also find that during times of struggle, I recite the word of God. Meditating on the word of God has made the word of God a powerful presence in my life.

CHAPTER 34

GOD MUST BE FIRST

"You shall have no other gods before me."
Exodus 20:3

God must be first in our lives. Sounds simple enough and yet it is so difficult for us. Some of our other gods are so very subtle that we don't even notice them. They are gods, though. We need to remove them from our hearts.

Abraham had to be willing to sacrifice his son. Joseph had to be willing as a slave and as a prisoner to put the needs of others first. Moses walked away from Pharaoh's court. Jonathan walked away from being king. Jesus went to the cross.

Daniel, Meshach, Shadrach and Abednego faced death rather than submit to the king's edicts. David did not slay King Saul when given the opportunity. Paul suffered beatings, shipwrecks, stonings and imprisonment. Rahab hid the spies. Esther approached the king. Stephen was stoned to death. Jesus went to the cross.

Fortunately, many of us will never face such challenges to our faith. Our challenges will be much more subtle. Jesus said:

> *"No one can serve two masters; for either he will hate*
> *the one and love the other, or he will hold to one and*
> *despise the other. You cannot serve God and mammon."*
> Matthew 6:24

Mammon is translated money. However, I apply the verse to everything in my life. I cannot serve it and God.

The verse is not telling us that money is evil. The evil is when money becomes first in our lives. King Solomon was the richest king of his day. God blesses us with riches. The problem is when the riches come before God. A poor man as well as a rich man can fall prey to this god. The poor man through his craving of it and the rich man through his hoarding of it. Both can also be content in the station to which God has called them in their service to Him first.

The verse is telling us that God must be first before everything and everyone else in our lives. God will ask us to give up things as He becomes first in our lives.

My first goal in life was to work as an engineer at NASA. I was doing it when God asked me to walk away. I walked away. Doing what God wanted was more important than my goal. I knew I could not truly be happy if I was out of God's will.

I did not think I did anything special, I just did what God asked me to do. Others, however, saw me walking away from something that I worked hard to obtain and financial security.

Jesus tells us:

> *"Truly I say to you, there is no one who has left house*
> *or wife or brothers or parents or children, for the sake of*
> *the kingdom of God, who shall not receive many times as*
> *much at this time and in the age to come, eternal life."*
> Luke 18:29, 30

The critical test of whether something is a god in our lives is the willingness to leave it behind in obedience to God's call. I had to do that when I walked away from my opportunities as an engineer and became a missionary. My family disapproved of my decision. Many of my friends disapproved. I knew in my heart it was what God wanted me to do.

Each time I have moved in response to God's call, people have questioned how I could start over. My answer has always been that it is what God wants me to do. I answer to Him.

Before I give the impression that God is always first in my life, I need to confess that I struggle with other gods in my life. They may not be obvious to others, but God knows they are there and He works in me. I usually don't recognize the other gods in my life until God points them out. It is amazing what can distract me from having God first in my life.

You are probably wondering what subtleties. How about the subtlety of faith? Is my faith in my faith or in God? The quantity of my faith is insignificant. The object of my faith is significant. God needs to remind me that it is His faithfulness, not my faith.

There is the subtlety of prayer. Ever heard the comments: he/she really knows how to pray; I wish I could pray like him/her; God answers his/her prayer. Does God answer his/her prayer or honor his/her heart? God wants first place in our hearts. He wants us to pray to Him so our concerns do not replace Him as first in our lives. People start to believe more in their prayers than God.

Here is my favorite subtlety: but who will take care of him/her if I don't? Now, we are playing god for that person's life. God can take care of them without us. That is hard to believe I know. We think only we love them enough to take care of them. God loves them more.

The saddest to me is when a person's ministry becomes their god. I fear many a missionary is prone to this one. It is not our ministry. It is the Lord's ministry. How often do we not have time for God because our ministry needs our attention? Ouch.

Shall I continue?

Even Christ did not consider Himself first. He did not consider it His ministry. His faith was not in His prayer. God, His Father, was first in His life.

I believe faith, prayer and ministry are part of the Christian's life. I believe service to others is important. Knowing the word of God is essential. God, however, must be first in the Christian life.

We shall have no other gods before Him. Anything other than God that becomes first in our lives is an idol. The thing we are anxious for can become an idol if we do not turn it over to God. I think that is why the Apostle Paul tells us:

> *"Be anxious for nothing, but in everything by prayer*
> *and supplication with thanksgiving let your requests*
> *be made known to God. And the peace of God,*
> *which surpasses all comprehension, shall guard*
> *your hearts and your minds in Christ Jesus."*
> *Philippians 4:6, 7*

By giving those things that occupy our minds and hearts to God, our hearts are guarded in their relationship to Jesus. Giving them to God, keeps God first in our lives. I close by sharing these verses again:

> *"fixing our eyes on Jesus, the author*
> *and perfecter of faith."*
> *Hebrews 12:2*

CHAPTER 35

LIFELONG WALK

*"Not that I have already obtained it, or have already
become perfect, but I press on in order that I may
lay hold of that for which also I was laid hold of
by Christ Jesus. Brethren, I do not regard myself
as having laid hold of it yet; but one thing I do:
forgetting what lies behind and reaching forward to
what lies ahead, I press on toward the goal for the
prize of the upward call of God in Christ Jesus."*
Philippians 3:12-14

God's walk with us is lifelong. Like the Apostle Paul, we must press on. The lessons I have learned and shared are ongoing lessons. The wilderness is only part of the journey.

Abraham and Moses were adults when they entered the wilderness. Jacob and Joseph were teenagers. The wilderness journey was different for each of them, as it will be different for each of us.

The goal is not the journey. The goal is faith in God. People often think the goal is to become Christ like. I believe the goal is faith in God and becoming Christ like is a result of faith.

God's walk with us is about faith in the Being of Jesus Christ, not about being like Jesus Christ. There is a difference.

God's walk with us is not about the fulfillment of promises, but about faith in the Promise Maker. Abraham, Jacob, Joseph and Moses did not see the promise of a Messiah, Jesus Christ, fulfilled. Daniel, Meshach, Shadrach and Abednego did not see the promise fulfilled. None of the prophets or the servants of the Old Testament saw the promise fulfilled, but they did have faith in the Promise Maker.

The Apostle Paul says:

> *"More than that, I count all things to be loss in view of the surpassing value of knowing Christ Jesus my Lord, for whom I have suffered the loss of all things, and count them but rubbish in order that I may gain Christ, and may be found in Him, not having a righteousness of my own derived from the Law, but that which is through faith in Christ, the righteousness which comes from God on the basis of faith, that I may know Him, and the power of His resurrection and the fellowship of His sufferings, being conformed to His death; in order that I may attain to the resurrection from the dead."*
> *Philippians 3:8-11*

There are several important truths that Paul states:

- Value of knowing Christ
- May gain Christ
- A righteousness that is through faith in Christ
- A righteousness that comes from God on the basis of faith
- Know Him
- Know the power of His resurrection
- Know the fellowship of His sufferings

- Being conformed to His death
- May attain to the resurrection from the dead

Paul's goal was to know Christ. His goal was to have faith in Christ. His goal was to experience Christ to the fullness of Christ's experiences. His hope was the resurrection from the dead.

As the believers of the Old Testament looked forward to the fulfillment of the promise, Paul looked forward to the fulfillment of the promise. Yes, Jesus Christ the Messiah has come. Our hope is His resurrected life in us. Our faith is in Him.

It is a difficult task to keep our eyes fixed on Jesus (Hebrews 12:2) as the writer of Hebrews encourages us to do. There is so much to grab our attention. There is so much we are taught to do as Christians. God only asks one thing of us. God asks us to have faith in His Son, Jesus Christ. He will accomplish the rest.

The Psalmist wrote:

> *"The Lord will accomplish what concerns me."*
> *Psalms 138:8*

The Apostle Paul wrote:

> *"For we are His workmanship, created in Christ*
> *Jesus for good works, which God prepared*
> *beforehand, that we should walk in them."*
> *Ephesians 2:10*

The Lord will accomplish us becoming who we are in Christ. We are His workmanship. We don't become by our efforts. We become by faith in God who does the work. He is the author of our faith. We need to look to Him and trust Him.

It is so simple and yet so difficult. What did Paul write in Philippians 3:13 and 14? He said he had not yet arrived but he pressed on. It is a lifelong journey. There will be victories along the way, there will be losses along the way, there will be time to rest along the way and at all times God will be walking with us. Matthew closes his gospel with these final words of Jesus:

> *"and lo, I am with you always, even to the end of the age."*
> *Matthew 28:20*

CHAPTER 36

CLOSING THOUGHTS

"Brethren, I do not regard myself as having laid
hold of it yet; but one thing I do: forgetting what
lies behind and reaching forward to what lies
ahead. I press on toward the goal for the prize
of the upward call of God in Christ Jesus."
Philippians 3:13, 14

As I reflect on what has been written on these pages, I am struck with the fact that there is so much more of God than I know. God is not a perfect man. God is not the most powerful king. God is God!

As children of God, we are blessed to be known by Him and to know Him. People often ask if you could meet one person in the world who would you want to meet? While I have an answer, knowing God is so much more thrilling.

God chose us. I am amazed when I contemplate that God chose me. Of all the people He could choose, He chose me.

He blesses us. The God of the universe blesses us. The God of the universe cares about us. The God of the universe wants what is best for us.

God is faithful to us. Over and over again, as we study biblical characters, we see the faithfulness of God. We give God so many reasons to walk away from us, but He stays faithful to us. He stays faithful because He promised to be faithful. Meditate on God's faithfulness; it is overwhelming.

The Christian life is difficult. We don't talk about the difficulties enough. It scares us to think someone is struggling. Struggling is part of the Christian life. Our cloud of witnesses struggled.

Until that day when we see Christ as He can be fully known, as the Apostle Paul said, we need to press on. I want to fully know the power of Christ in my life. I want you to fully know the power of Christ in your life.

I close with the benediction from the book of Hebrews:

> *"Now the God of peace, who brought up from the dead*
> *the great Shepherd of the sheep through the blood of*
> *the eternal covenant, even Jesus our Lord, equip you*
> *in every good thing to do His will, working in us that*
> *which is pleasing in His sight, through Jesus Christ,*
> *to whom be the glory forever and ever. Amen."*
> *Hebrews 13:20, 21*

SAVING FAITH

"What will a man be profited, if he gains the whole world, and forfeits his soul (Matthew 16:26)?"

CHAPTER 2

INTRODUCTION

When talking about God walking with us, it is essential that we have a saving faith in Christ. It is this relationship with Christ that is of concern. If you have not placed your faith in Christ, I hope the truth of a Saving Faith opens your heart to Christ. If you have placed your faith in Christ, I hope this truth strengthens your faith and helps you share your saving faith with others.

As in any relationship, there are a few things we learn about the individual and how they relate before we make a 'true' commitment to the relationship. Well, the same is true for us to make a commitment of saving faith in Christ and have a relationship with God the Father through Christ. There are a few fundamental Biblical truths that need to be known and believed.

In order to truly have a saving faith in Christ, in order for a Christian to truly have a relationship with God the Father, he/she needs to believe that God exists and He has spoken, sin exists, the penalty for sin exists, and Christ's finished work exists. An individual needs to understand that there is the problem of sin in one's relationship with God and saving faith in Christ is the only solution.

We are called Christians because in Christ we are partakers of His finished work. We have saving faith in Christ's finished work to heal our broken relationship with our God.

God walking with us does not make sense without understanding the relationship a believer has with God the Father through Jesus Christ. My goal is not to provide a theological debate concerning these spiritual truths, but to provide the reader an understanding of saving faith in Christ. Everything we have as Christians, we have because of Christ. It is in His finished work.

CHAPTER 3

GOD EXISTS AND HE HAS SPOKEN

It astounds me that people can deny the existence of God. How can a person look at the world around him/her and not believe in God is beyond me. Now, people who do not believe in God feel the same way about me.

My first response to them, however, is that if God does not exist, I have not lost anything by believing. If God does exist, they have lost everything by not believing.

Creation begs belief in a Creator. We exist. An apologetic I like to use with doubters to explain the need for a God for our own existence is:

1. Something exists.
2. Something cannot come from nothing.
3. Therefore, for something to exist, something has to have already existed always.

For me, as a believer, that something that has always existed is the God of the Bible. I believe the Bible is the inerrant Word of God.

I believe in the God of the Bible. I believe God exists and that He is spoken through His written Word, the Bible, and through His living Word, Jesus Christ.

Being a Christian requires a belief in God and that He has spoken. The Book of John, Chapter 1 verses 1- 18 reads:

> "In the beginning was the Word, and the Word was with God, and the Word was God. He was in the beginning with God. All things came into being by Him, and apart from Him nothing came into being that has come into being. In Him, was life, and the life was the light of men...But as many as received Him, to them He gave the right to become children of God, even to those who believe in His name, who were born not of blood, nor of the will of the flesh, nor of the will of man, but of God. And the Word became flesh, and dwelt among us, and we beheld His glory, glory as of the only begotten from the Father, full of grace and truth...For of His fulness we have all received, and grace upon grace. For the law was given through Moses; grace and truth were realized through Jesus Christ. No man has seen God at any time; the only begotten God, who is in the bosom of the Father, He has explained Him."

One cannot have faith as a Christian apart from the word of God. God exists and He has spoken. He is His Word. A common expression use to be that a man was only as good as his word and the word of a good man was all you needed.

God is as good as His word. And His Word, Jesus Christ, is all we need to have a right relationship with our God; for God to walk with us.

I remember a sharing experience I had with a college student. Her comment was that because she did not know God, He could not exist. My comment to her was that a few moments ago she did not know me and yet I existed. I explained to her that her knowledge of me was not necessary for my existence.

I went on to point out that a lot of people in this world exist without her knowledge of them. None of us need her knowledge of us for our existence.

I further explained that God exists with or without her knowledge of Him. The bigger question was, "Does she want to know God?"

Do you want to know God?

Do you want God to walk with you?

CHAPTER 4

EXISTENCE OF SIN

The first few chapters of the Book of Genesis tell the story of creation (yes, I believe the story) and the introduction of sin. In Genesis 2:17, God clearly tells Adam,

> "but from the tree of the knowledge of good and evil you shall not eat, for in the day that you eat from it you shall surely die."

Well, Adam and Eve ate the fruit from the tree of good and evil and Genesis 3:7 tells us

> "then the eyes of both of them were opened and they knew that they were naked; and they sewed fig leaves together and made themselves loin coverings."

After eating the fruit, Adam and Eve felt shame, which means they felt guilt about their actions - they were experiencing feelings resulting from their sin. What is sin? It is disobeying a command given by the Lord. Adam and Eve disobeyed by the eating of the fruit.

The disobedience started in their hearts. The eating was the action that followed the heart's desire for the fruit. Their hearts wanted what they wanted more than what God wanted. And thus, they sinned.

One consequence of the sin is that Adam and Eve can no longer be naked with one another. Sin against God impacted their relationship with one another.

A second consequence, and a more critical one, is that it impacted their relationship with God; continuing in Genesis 3:8,

> "And they heard the sound of the Lord God walking
> in the garden in the cool of the day, and the man
> and his wife hid themselves from the presence of the
> Lord God among the trees of the garden."

Adam and Eve hid from God. God walked with them and talked with them and now they are hiding. Their relationship with God was forever changed. Man's relationship with God was forever changed. There is now spiritual separation in the relationship between God and man.

Don't get too upset with Adam and Eve because we too are sinners and sin every day. And yes, I believe any one of us given the choice given Adam and Eve would have done the same thing and eaten of the fruit.

Romans 3:23 tells us,

> "for all have sinned and fall short of the glory
> of God."

It is very clear from this verse that we are all sinners and all fall short of the glory of God. It isn't just the vile among us, but all of us.

History is filled with the hateful sins of humanity. We are sinners. If you think you are perfect and without sin, just ask a few people who know you well and they will be able to point out your flaws.

Sin exists in our hearts.

Do you grasp that you are a sinner?

CHAPTER 5

PENALTY FOR SIN

I want to take a little time here for reflection. Remember in Genesis 2:17 that God says in that day you shall surely die. However, Adam and Eve did not physically die. So, what happened?

What kind of dying was God predicting? I believe God was predicting a spiritual death; spiritual separation from God. They hid from God, they experienced a brokenness in their relationship with God. Adam and Eve died a spiritual death - they knew they were naked.

The penalty for sin is spiritual death. It is a spiritual brokenness in man's relationship with His Creator. We often think about our physical death, but I believe it's the spiritual death that is of significance. Man was created to have fellowship with his creator. When man sinned that fellowship was broken.

It is important that we reflect on the impact sin has on our relationship with God. We often sweep our little 'sins' under the rug as part of being human. And yes, it is part of being a sinful human. But those little sins keep us from enjoying fellowship with our God and do need to be addressed. Fortunately, as we will discuss in the next chapter, God provided a solution for our sins and the penalty for them.

Our physical death also is a result of the sin. Please read Genesis 3:22-24,

> "Then the Lord God said, "Behold, the man has become like one of Us, knowing good and evil; and now, lest he stretch out his hand, and take also from the tree of life, and eat, and live forever" - therefore the Lord God sent him out from the garden of Eden, to cultivate the ground from which he was taken. So He drove the man out; and at the east of the garden of Eden He stationed the cherubim, and the flaming sword which turned every direction, to guard the way to the tree of life."

I believe physical death was God having mercy on us from having to live in this body of sin for eternity. God guarded the way to the tree of life so man would not live forever in a state of sin.

In Christ, we have the hope that one day we will be with Him in heaven and free from this condition of sin. That is a glorious thought. And Christ confirms that He is our path to a relationship with the Father in John 14:6,

> "Jesus said to him, 'I am the way, and the truth, and the life; no one comes to the Father, but through me.'"

The way back to the tree of life, a spiritual life, is through Christ. In Christ, we have a spiritual life with the Father for eternity. In Romans 6:23 we read,

> "For the wages of sin is death, but the free gift of God is eternal life in Christ Jesus our Lord."

In keeping with my thought above, the wages of sin is spiritual death; a life apart from God. The eternal life in Christ is a spiritual life; a life with a relationship with God for eternity.

The penalty for sin is spiritual death. It isn't the penalty for some sin and not other sin, but the penalty for all sin is death.

In our justice system, the penalty for committing a crime is dependent on the severity of the crime. In God's justice system, there is only one penalty for any and all sin...spiritual death.

Apart from Christ we cannot enjoy a relationship with our Creator and God; He will not walk with us. It is not a separation from society with visitation rights. There are no visitation rights and it is complete separation from God. It is a very severe sentence and the sentence is for eternity!

Repeating Romans 3:23, "all have sinned and fall short of the glory of God." We all have sinned and deserve the death sentence. However, there is the finished work of Christ which saves those who believe.

CHAPTER 6

FINISHED WORK
OF CHRIST

We often like to think that if we do enough good things, it will wipe away any of the bad things we have done. We are not seeking forgiveness for our sin. We are seeking a goodness that outweighs the badness. However, that does not address our sin.

There is a direct penalty for our sin. Death is required for God to extend forgiveness to the sinner. Blood must be shed.

God has demanded the death of an innocent one. God has demanded the sprinkling of blood of the one who dies as payment for the one who sins. Apart from the death payment, a man's sins cannot be forgiven.

In the Old Testament, the Israeli nation was constantly providing innocent animals for blood offerings for the sin of individuals and for the sin of the nation. The life of the animals was in the blood. So ultimately, what God was requiring was the sacrifice of the life of the innocent animal for the life of the guilty sinner. God was requiring an innocent life be sacrificed unto death for the forgiveness of sins.

I believe we can say the first sacrifice for man's sin occurred in Genesis 3:21 when we read,

> "And the Lord God made garments of skin for
> Adam and his wife, and clothed them."

Innocent blood was shed to cover man's nakedness (shame, sin).

The problem is that the sacrifice of animals never fully satisfied the penalty for sins and so needed to be constantly offered. The priest would sprinkle the sinner with the blood as a sign that the penalty for his sin had been borne by the innocent animal. However, the sprinkling of animal blood did not last. It was only a symbol for the real sacrifice that would be paid for our sins which was the death of the Son of God, Jesus Christ.

God planned for the ultimate sacrifice for the forgiveness of our sins. God planned to satisfy the penalty of spiritual death once and for all, so that we could have a relationship with the God of the Bible, our Creator and Father. God planned to walk with us again in the gardens of our lives.

Christ's sacrificial death was the plan and fulfills that penalty for our sin. He was without blemish. He was without flaw. He was without sin. He is the Son of God who takes away the sin of the world. John 1:29 reads,

> "The next day he saw Jesus coming to him, and said,
> "Behold, the Lamb of God who takes away the sin
> of the world!""

I believe there were two deaths experienced by Christ on the cross. There was the painful physical death of the crucifixion. And, there was the painful spiritual death or spiritual separation from God the Father when Christ proclaimed in Matthew 27:46,

> "My God, My God, why hast Thou forsaken Me?"

The physical death was the innocent blood for the forgiveness of our sins. Through Christ's physical death on the cross there was the shedding of innocent blood. When God looks at us, as believers, He sees the blood of Christ shed on our behalf and we are forgiven.

But remember, I believe the penalty of sin was spiritual death; and through that moment of spiritual death experienced by Christ on the cross, the penalty for sin was satisfied.

Both deaths were necessary; innocent blood needed to be shed and the penalty needed to be paid. Both were accomplished in the One, Jesus Christ.

Think on this: The Son of God, for a moment in time (the gospels of Mark and Luke tell us that this moment lasted for three hours) was separated from God the Father, in order that we might have eternal life; that we might spend eternity with God the Father. It was the ultimate sacrifice.

Christ's work did not end with dying on a cross. Christ rose from the dead. Christ demonstrated that there was life after death, and that life was ours in Him. Christ proved that he had power over death. Christ demonstrated that he had the power to give us life; spiritual life.

Christ ascended into heaven; He showed us where we would ultimately live for eternity. And after Christ ascended, the Spirit of God descended upon us as believers. As believers we are not alone to live out the Christian life, but we have the Spirit of God in us. Christ not only purchased our forgiveness of sin but, through the Holy Spirit, gives us the power to sin no more.

It is an overwhelming thought. I am still in awe that God did all that for me. He did all that for you. He did all that so He could walk with us.

CHAPTER 7

CLOSING THOUGHTS

God walking with us involves growing in our relationship with God the Father and learning to become overcomers in our struggle between our inane ability to sin and the power of the Holy Spirit of God within us as we seek to serve the Lord and to sin no more. But first, we need to be sure we are ready for the walk.

Do you believe God exists?

Do you believe you are a sinner?

Do you understand the penalty of your sin? Do you understand that you pay the penalty for your sin (eternal separation from God) or you accept the payment Christ completed on the cross?

Have you placed your faith in Christ? If you should die and come before God, and He asked you why He should let you into heaven, are you able to say because of what Christ did on the cross? If God was to ask me, my answer would be because of who I am in Christ. Christ paid the penalty for my sin. He purchased eternal life for me.

The title of this section is "Saving Faith." Someone who has placed his/her faith in Christ, a Christian, believes in the God of the Bible, repents of sin, accepts Christ's death for the forgiveness of sins, accepts Christ as Lord of one's life and submits to the Spirit of God to continue his/her life journey in Christ. And, it is a life journey with God walking with us.

If you have already placed your faith in Christ, I hope this book encourages you in your walk with Him. If you have not placed your faith in Christ, I offer this prayer for you to say so that you too can enjoy the fullness of God's love for you, the forgiveness of your sin, and know the power of the Spirit of God in your life; that you may begin your life journey in Christ with God walking with you.

Dear Lord, I acknowledge my sin. I acknowledge my inability to do anything about the penalty for my sin. I acknowledge by faith that Christ on the cross paid the penalty for my sin. By faith I place my life in Your hands. I ask that Christ be Lord of my life. I accept His death and resurrection on my behalf. I ask the Spirit of God to take residence in my life and cause me to grow in the likeness of Christ to the glory of God. I ask You to walk with me. Amen.

In closing, Isaiah 12:2:

> "Behold, God is my salvation, I will trust and not be afraid; For the Lord God is my strength and song, and He has become my salvation."

ABOUT THE AUTHOR

Mary was a senior in college when she committed her life to the Lordship of Christ. Upon graduation, rather than pursue her engineering career, she became a missionary.

Often she was asked why she gave up the money and the opportunities offered her as a woman engineer. Her response was always that she did not give up anything. If God wanted her to be an engineer again one day, she would be.

Well, some twenty years later she was getting her Master's Degree in Engineering Management and her Professional Engineering License in Mechanical Engineering. Earlier she had received her Master's Degree in Counseling.

Mary would say the path she followed is the one God planned for her and that He has walked with her the whole way. One of her favorite comments is from *The Hiding Place* by Corrie Ten Boom – There are no ifs in the will of God.

She is retired now and is focusing on writing and ministry. She lives with family in Sacramento, CA.

Contact information:

Mlyon2004@gmail.com
www.HeWalksWithUs.com

Books by Mary L. Lyon

He Walks With Us
It is about how God takes His children by the hand,
walking with them in His love, forgiveness and truth.